T0127408

Do Scale

A road map to growing a remarkable company

Les McKeown

For Jen Gerasimas
An unparalleled mentor and coach, and an irreplaceable friend.

Published by
The Do Book Company 2019
Works in Progress Publishing Ltd
thedobook.co

To find out more about our company, books and authors, please visit **thedobook.co** or follow us **@dobookco**

5% of our proceeds from the sale of this book is given to The Do Lectures to help it achieve its aim of making positive change **thedolectures.com**

Cover designed by James Victore
Book designed and set by Ratiotype

Printed and bound by OZGraf Print on Munken, an FSC-certified paper

A CIP catalogue record for this book is available from the British Library

ISBN 978-1-907974-59-5

10 9 8 7 6 5 4 3 2

CONTENTS

INTRODUCTION

These days it seems that every business leader talks at some point about wanting to 'scale' their organisation, but most have a confused, unattainable and, frankly, plain wrong understanding of what this means — and what it entails. And those who do have some clarity on the matter seem to have no idea how to go about it.

In writing this book, I hope to not only clearly define what it means to scale an organisation (whether for-profit or not-for-profit), but also lay out the personal challenges facing the founder or leader who wants to scale, and provide a clear step-by-step road map they must follow in order to scale successfully and sustainably.

By reading this book, you will:

— Know what 'scaling' truly means and at what point in the business it is an option for you.

— Have the information you need to decide whether the implications of scaling your organisation is something you're prepared to personally commit to.

— Understand the behavioural, attitudinal and skill shifts you'll need to make as a leader if you are to scale up.

— Take away a step-by-step road map of the specific, mechanical steps you need to take to scale your organisation (and those people working within it).

— Have access to online resources that complement each chapter.

To help you navigate the book, I have divided it into three clear sections:

1. MEANING —— 2. MINDSET —— 3. ROAD MAP

The first part clarifies what we mean by 'scaling', including a specific definition that will be used in the rest of the book, and contrasts scaling with other forms of growth within a business. The second part explores the personal changes required to become a 'scalable leader', while the third and final part lays out a precise road map of the actual steps required to scale.

There are two final considerations before we get started.

1. HOW DO YOU KNOW THE TIME IS RIGHT FOR YOU?

As a founder, leader or entrepreneur, how do you know when the time is right to consider scaling your organisation? I'd say there are three indicators that the time is right for you. None of these are inviolable — if you truly want to, you can probably scale when only meeting one or two of the three points below — but if you meet all three, the time is most definitely right.

- **You're past the early 'startup' phase.** Getting a new venture off the ground has its own challenges, and it is important to focus on becoming viable first, before looking to scale. (I know, I know ... what about Amazon, and Facebook, and ... We'll see later in the book why the myth of the scalable startup is just that — a myth.)

- **You have strong cash flow.** As we'll see, scaling has financial implications — there are some investments you'll need to make, mostly in systems and processes. So, while I can't tell you precisely how much money you'll need in the bank to start down the road to scalability, you will at the very least benefit greatly if you are experiencing consistent positive cash flow.

- **Your market segment is strong and growing.** In terms of your organisation's ability to scale, the growth of the overall market segment you operate in will act either as a headwind (where you are battling low, slow or no growth in the overall market), or as a tailwind, accelerating your scalability with overall market growth. It's much easier to scale in a fast-growing market than in a sluggish one.

2. WHY SHOULD YOU LISTEN TO ME?

Why do I get to write this book? What entitles me to talk about scaling and scalability?

Very fair question. In a nutshell: experience and pattern recognition. After qualifying as a chartered accountant (the UK equivalent of a CPA), I became a serial entrepreneur (although we didn't have that term back then), launching over 40 businesses before I was 35. In my mid-career, I co-founded and managed one of the very first business incubation units (again, we didn't use that phrase back then), which grew over a decade into an international business growth consultancy, employing at its peak over 100 people in 13 offices world-wide.

Two decades ago, I sold my share in that company and moved to the US to study growth patterns in very large enterprises. After working with organisations such as Microsoft, American Express, the US Army, Harvard University, T-Mobile (now EE in the UK), United Technologies and Chevron, I distilled the patterns of growth and scalability that I had recognised and published *Predictable Success: Getting Your Organisation On the Growth Track — and Keeping It There*, which became a *Wall Street Journal* and *USA Today* bestseller, followed by *The Synergist: How to Lead Your Team to Predictable Success* and *Do Lead: Share your vision. Inspire others. Achieve the impossible.*

For the last 15 years, I have been coaching and consulting with leaders in both for-profit and not-for-profit organisations on how to successfully scale — and this book is the culmination of that work.

My hope is that you find it useful and it helps you navigate this new and exciting phase of your business. Enjoy!

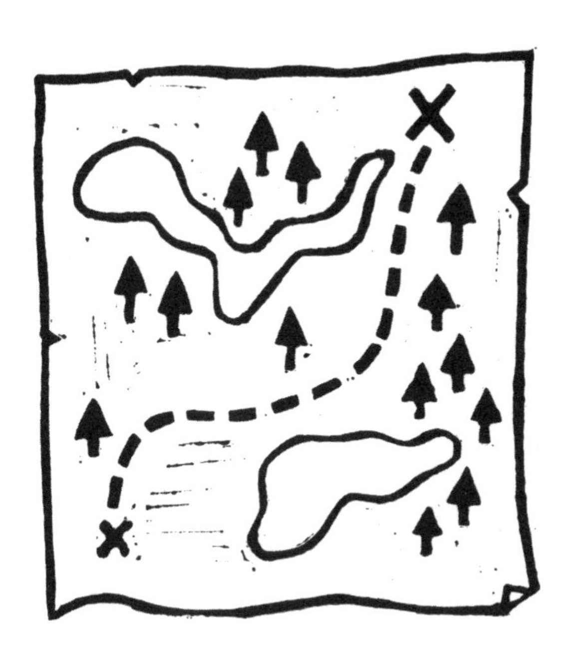

MEANING

In the first part of *Do Scale*, we will look closely at what it actually means to 'scale' an organisation; agree a definition to use throughout the rest of the book, and contrast scaling with other types of growth.

CHAPTER ONE
WHAT DOES IT REALLY MEAN TO 'SCALE'?

There's no better place to start than by defining our terms: what *exactly* do we mean when we talk about 'scale', 'scaling' and 'scalability'?

In this chapter:

— We'll look at the most common misconceptions and myths about what 'scaling' means in a business context.

— I'll provide a clear definition of 'scalability' that we can refer back to as we journey through the book and examine its implications.

— We'll turn our definition into a customised, motivating 'Scale Vision' written specifically for your organisation that will become your North Star as you and your team navigate your way to scale.

WHERE 'SCALING' COMES FROM

'Scaling up' was a common concept in engineering and referred to how well a system performs when significantly greater demands are placed upon it. Some decades ago the term crossed over from the world of engineering to business as we began to refer to companies 'scaling up' when talking generally about growth.

Soon commentators dropped the 'up', and now we talk about 'scaling'. If a new app comes onto the market, we might ask questions like, 'Do you think this product can scale?' Or we might be talking about an entire company — which is what we'll be looking at in this book. Unfortunately, as the use of the term has proliferated, the precision with which it is used has deteriorated to the point where we don't have a definition of scaling that is widely adopted and agreed.

WHAT 'SCALING' USUALLY MEANS

When you read something like: '[Company x] seems set to scale considerably over the next few years'; or 'The CEO told me he's totally focused on scaling our offering over the next three quarters', what do you think it means?

Usually, we have a vague response when someone talks about 'scaling', a general sense that they mean something like 'getting very big, very fast'.

If you were to probe your reaction a little deeper, you might find a few other assumptions lurking in there, such as:

- When we talk about scaling, we're primarily referring to *revenue*, not (necessarily) to profits. In other words, scaling happens at the top line.
- If someone is talking about scaling, we often assume they are running a startup.
- Scaling is something startups have to do, or they die.

— Scaling is different from 'growth'.

— Scaling is complicated and is certainly more challenging than 'growth', or wouldn't everyone be doing it?

— Scaling is not for the faint-hearted. Just as we talk about 'scaling' Mount Everest, so deciding to scale our organisation will be no walk in the park.

All of these hidden assumptions, while reasonable, are deceptive and, at a subconscious level, daunting. Without a clear, precise definition of scaling, we're left with not much more than a vague, incoherent sense of a somewhat mysterious type of super-growth, an all-consuming, high-energy company transformation equivalent to Bruce Banner turning into The Hulk.

As we're about to see, it doesn't need to be like that. While running any organisation is never quite a 'walk in the park', we *can* scale without it being a crippling, exhausting or mysterious process. And it all starts with being clear about what scaling means.

WHAT SCALING REALLY IS

For the rest of this book, I'd like for us instead to work on the basis of a clear, agreed definition, one that I've used for over 30 years, and has both stood the test of time and provided the key to unlocking 'scale' in organisations of all types over and over again. Are you ready? Here it is:

> **Scalability is the ability over time to sustainably grow your organisation to whatever size your industry or sector will allow, in whichever market segment(s) you choose to engage in.**

We'll dive deeper into each clause in our definition shortly, but first, let's note a couple of immediate takeaways.

Firstly, it defines *scalability*, not *scaling*. The difference is nuanced, but incredibly important — one is about a thing (scaling), the other (scalability) is about having the ability to do a thing.

Think of it this way. You're out walking when a skateboarder zooms past you at great speed. You can think one of two things: 'There goes someone on a skateboard.' Or, 'There goes someone who knows how to ride a skateboard.' The noise of a fall — clattering wood, wheels and a muffled swear word — indicates the difference between the two. It's one thing to be on a skateboard, and an entirely different thing to be able to ride it well.

In this book, we're interested in making sure your company has the ability to scale. That you control the scaling, not that it controls you.

Secondly, even with a clear definition to hand, some aspects of scaling will differ from organisation to organisation. We will identify those differences and, before you finish this chapter, you'll write your own customised definition of what it means to scale.

Let's look at our definition in more detail.

'The ability over time to sustainably *grow* …'

Let's not beat about the bush: at its most basic, to 'scale' is to grow. To be specific, scaling is a particular subset of growth possessing its own unique characteristics, as the rest of our definition will affirm and expand upon.

For now, however, let's agree on this important distinction: while scaling is a type of growth, not all growth is scaling!

'The ability over time to *sustainably* grow …'

Here's the first element of distinction between scaling and

other forms of organisational growth. As we're defining it in this book, scaling is a form of *sustainable* growth.

That means we're not talking about, for example, artificially inflating a company's market share to attract additional investment (or to sell the company at an inflated value) or growing at such a headlong rate that it jeopardises the organisation's existence. We'll examine this distinction in more detail in chapters 2 and 3 when we compare scaling to initial, early-stage growth and/or artificially boosting market share for the purposes of attracting either investment or acquisition.

'The ability *over time* to sustainably grow ...'

As with any smart goals, achieving scalability should be time-bound. As we shall see throughout the rest of this book, successfully scaling a business isn't just a question of 'hitting and hoping' — it's a precise process, which you should be able to achieve over a fixed time period (we'll get around to estimating that time frame a little later in the book).

'... your organisation ...'

As I've already mentioned in the introduction, the ability to scale is not restricted to for-profit businesses. Whether you run a commercial enterprise on a large or small scale, a not-for-profit such as a faith- or cause-based organisation, a charity, a foundation or even an NGO, if you comprise a group of two or more people pursuing a common goal, then you're in. You can scale what you're doing.

'... to whatever size your industry or sector will allow ...'

The total market demand of, say, the bottled water industry is different from the size of, say, the framed poster industry. A not-for-profit looking for a cure for cancer is cooperating in a different-sized sector than a local refuge for single mothers. Given these size distinctions, the ability to scale means being able to put your foot on the accelerator and grow to whatever size your industry or sector will allow.

'... in whichever market segment(s) you choose to engage in.'

Few organisations 'scale to global' right from the get-go. The most common sequence is to first conquer whatever your 'local' market is, then regional, then national, then global. If your organisation is doing something virtual (like designing and selling apps, or trying to find a cure for cancer), then your market segments may be virtual, rather than geographic (as an app designer, you may choose initially to cater only to the English-language market, for example).

The important thing to realise is that scaling doesn't automatically mean getting as big as conceivably possible — you can scale to whatever market segments you choose to play in at any given time.

HOW TO USE THIS DEFINITION TO DEFINE SCALABILITY IN AND FOR YOUR ORGANISATION

It doesn't take much to turn our generic definition of scalability into an organisation-specific statement that summarises precisely what scaling means to you.

Here's an example. First, let's remind ourselves of the generic definition from earlier in this chapter:

> **Scalability is the ability over time to sustainably grow your organisation to whatever size your industry or sector will allow, in whichever market segment(s) you choose to engage in.**

Now let's see which parts of the definition need to be tweaked to specifically address your organisation. There are four of them, and I've indicated them in brackets below:

> **Scalability is the ability [over time] to sustainably grow [your organisation] to [whatever size your industry or sector will allow], in [whichever market segment(s) you choose to engage in].**

Let's take each in turn and, for reasons that will become obvious, we're going to address them in reverse order.

'Whichever market segments you choose to engage in'

Start by making an explicit commitment to the market segment(s) you want to scale into.

Let's say you have three highly successful coffee shops with a unique brand that everyone tells you (and you're convinced) can scale. Do you want to start by scaling locally (sounds like you already have that covered), regionally, nationally or internationally?

Remember: this isn't a choice for all time, it's just your North Star for the first iteration of scaling — you might decide to scale regionally for now, then when you've cracked that, come back and re-read *Do Scale* to scale nationally!

Identifying your market segments may be a little harder work if you run a not-for-profit, but it's important nonetheless. If you want to scale a church, for example, do you want to scale in geographical segments (local, regional, national, international) and/or do you want to scale in specific ministries (children's, worship, discipleship, etc.).

For your charity or foundation, again, geography may be relevant (where do you want to do the work you do?), but specific segments of your 'market' might be too — perhaps to begin with you only want to work with a certain age group or demographic.

The important thing is to be very clear about which specific market segments you want to scale into.

'Whatever size your industry or sector will allow'

While there is no compulsion to grow to the maximum size your industry or sector will allow, we're talking about the ability to do so if you wish (or if significant demands are made upon your organisation so that you have to!) or to grow to any point up to that maximum.

Think of the elevators in an office building — there's no need for you to press the button for the top floor when you get in, but you want the elevator to be able to take you there — and all the floors in between — as you choose.

Now, to what size will your industry or sector allow you to grow? That's where you'll have to do the hard work and burn some midnight oil working at your laptop.

In the first instance, Googling 'how to estimate market size' will give you a plethora of starting points.

'Your organisation'

Um, enter your organisation's name here. Don't say I pointed that out.

'Over time'

It's important to set a reasonable time frame in which to attain your scalability goals. While this doesn't need to be set in stone, it will give you a goal to work towards. Again, we'll get specific about the likely time frame later in the book — for now, enter what seems reasonable to you, as a placeholder.

Here are a couple of worked examples for you to model your Scale Vision on:

> 'We will scale Briggs Breeches to $175m in revenues over the next three years, serving the North American men's pants market, including the USA and Canada.'

> 'Over the next five years, we will scale the Grenville House Refuge Charity for Single Mothers by opening 35 homes throughout the United Kingdom, serving single, homeless mothers under the age of 25.'

Now, have a go at writing your own here:

Got your own Scale Vision? Great. Let's set about making it happen!

SUMMARY: CHAPTER 1

— 'Scaling' was originally developed as a term used in engineering.

— We usually have a vague sense of what we mean by 'scaling' — typically something like 'getting very big, very fast'.

— For the purposes of this book, we will use a specific definition: *'Scalability is the ability over time to sustainably grow your organisation to whatever size your industry or sector will allow, in whichever market segment(s) you choose to engage in.'*

— Note that our definition focuses on scalability, not just the act of scaling.

— You can (and should) use the definition to develop your own Scale Vision — a succinct, one- or two-sentence summary explaining what scaling means for your own organisation. This will act as your North Star.

Please go to **DoScaleBook.com** to see additional resources associated with this topic.

CHAPTER TWO
SCALE VERSUS GROWTH

So now we have defined what scalability is: essentially the ability to grow a business in a planned way to achieve defined goals. In this chapter, we will look at how we can begin to achieve this. We will also look at the difference between scaling an organisation (achieving exponential growth) and what might be termed linear or 'organic' growth, which is what you've been doing so far to build your business.

The basic difference between scaling and mere 'growth' can be seen immediately from the illustration below:

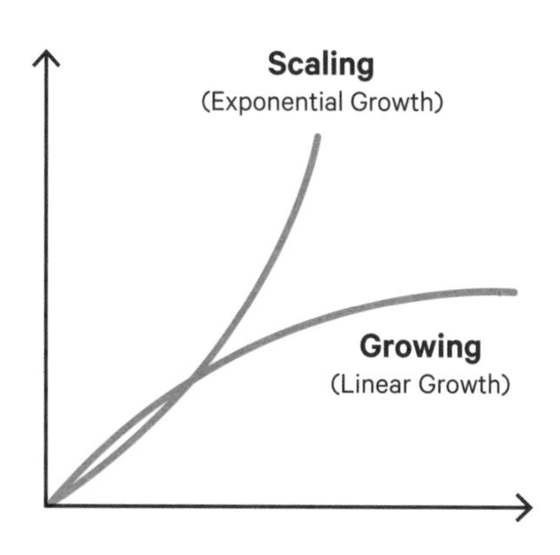

You can see that while linear ('organic') growth produces a steady rise along the vertical axis, *scaling* produces an even more dramatic rise — sometimes referred to as a 'J-curve' (the 'J' doesn't stand for anything — it's just because the shape of the curve looks like a J). The Hockey Stick is also a popular analogy.

WHAT ARE WE MEASURING?

To clarify: what are we measuring in the graph above?

Well, the horizontal axis is easy — it's growth over time. The vertical axis, on the other hand, could be any number of things: top-line revenues; how profitable you are; number of employees; market capitalization ... there is a wide variety of ways in which we could measure scale versus growth.

Thankfully, things are simplified for us by our core definition from Chapter 1:

> **Scalability is the ability over time to sustainably grow your organisation to whatever size your industry or sector will allow, in whichever market segment(s) you choose to engage in.**

Defining scalability in this way means that market share is the most appropriate metric to use for the vertical axis. So let's look at our graph again, this time with labels:

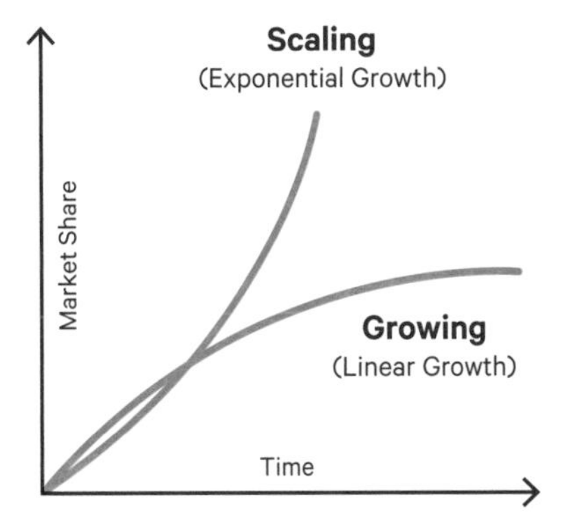

Let's dive a little deeper into what's going on here. To be specific: what, precisely, do we mean when we talk about scaling via exponential growth, and how is that different from linear growth?

WHAT IS EXPONENTIAL GROWTH?

Let's start with a simple definition of exponential growth that flows naturally from the x and y axes of our graph above:

> **Exponential growth is achieved by maximising market share over the shortest achievable time span.**

This is simple, and elegant, and almost serves our purpose, but we need to make one tweak in order to sync with our core definition of scalability. You will recall that definition includes a reference to sustainability, and so should this:

> **Exponential growth is that which is achieved by** ***sustainably*** **maximising market share over the shortest achievable time span.**

WHAT IS LINEAR (ORGANIC) GROWTH?

Linear growth is essentially any form of growth that's not exponential:

> **Linear growth is that which is achieved in any manner *other than* through a primary focus on maximising market share over time.**

This is the way most organisations grow — with a primary focus that isn't on radically increasing market share, but is on one or more of any number of other potential goals such as profitability, asset growth, quality of life, employee satisfaction or product quality.

THE CONSTRAINTS OF HAVING A PRIMARY FOCUS

The key distinction between an organisation that is scaling and one that is not comes down to its primary focus: maximising market share versus ... well, anything else.

Does this mean that an organisation committed to scaling cannot achieve any of those other goals? No. It just means that (with one exception) it cannot make any of them a *primary* focus of the business.

This is because an organisation that has committed itself to scaling has (by our definition) already chosen its primary focus — maximising market share in the shortest time possible — and, by definition, you can only have one primary focus. So, with effort, and if the organisation's leadership works hard at it, other goals can indeed be achieved (like employee satisfaction, for example), but they will always be subservient to the primary focus of sustainably maximising market share in the shortest time possible.

There is one exception to this exclusivity of primary focus, and it comes about because of a word we've mentioned a number of times already: sustainability.

If you want to scale *sustainably* (and if you don't, save yourself a bunch of time by jumping to Chapter 3) you can't increase market share at any cost. There will always be one other parameter — let's call it the *sustainability parameter* — you will have to fulfil.

For a commercial enterprise, the sustainability parameter is obvious and compelling: it's *profitability*. Increasing market share without profitability will mean the business will eventually die — that's the rule of capitalism (again, we'll talk about short-term exceptions to this rule in Chapter 3: Scaling versus Flipping).

If you run a not-for-profit, then your sustainability parameter may not be called 'profitability' — you might refer to a 'surplus' or 'positive cash flow' — but whatever you call it (and however you attain it, whether through fund-raisers, grants, memberships or donations) it still needs to be met if your scalability is to last.

PLANNED VERSUS UNPLANNED EXPONENTIAL GROWTH

One final distinction before we move on.

Organisations can scale in two ways: planned or unplanned. Planned growth is just that. The leadership team makes a commitment to scaling and sets a strategy in progress to get there. That, in essence, is the subject of this book.

Unplanned exponential growth is a different thing altogether. In this scenario, the leadership team may not have been pursuing scale at all, but suddenly it finds demand far outweighs supply. Maybe a celebrity was photographed carrying one of your handbags. Head over to *DoScaleBook.com* to see some examples on the accompanying website.

Here, the exponential growth brought by unplanned scale can have a crushing impact on the business, suddenly doubling, tripling, quadrupling the volume of business month by month (or week by week, in extreme cases). Not being ready for a sudden high demand for a product or service can have a catastrophic effect on a business — and its employees.

The good news is that the road map laid out in this book will prepare you for either event. So read on to ensure you have the strategy you need at hand, should you be fortunate enough to have exponential growth knocking on your door.

EXPONENTIAL OR LINEAR GROWTH: WHICH DO YOU WANT?

Okay, now you know the basic difference between the two types of growth (exponential growth — scaling — with its focus on maximising market share; and linear, organic growth), it's time to make your first choice. Which do you want?

The answer to this question may seem obvious to you. 'Les,' you're saying, 'I didn't buy a book called *Do Scale* just out of academic interest :-)'

I get it, but humour me. Go back and re-read this chapter, particularly the sections that contrast the different primary focus of those organisations committed to scale (i.e. maximising market share), and those that are not.

Rethink your commitment to scale in the light of that decision to maximise market share as your primary focus.

Is that what you truly want? Or would you prefer to be able to remain primarily focused on other areas — like personal work-life balance, or giving back to the community, or simply providing the highest quality product or service possible?

Now, to be clear, I'm not saying that if you decide to scale you can't also have any of these other things — it's just that you can't make them your *primary focus.*

Let me give you an example. Some years ago, I was working with a luthier — that's the technical name for someone who makes guitars. His guitars were so good, and became so well known, that he woke up one day and realised that he had in fact morphed into becoming the owner of a guitar-manufacturing business — one that was showing every sign that it could scale appreciably.

Well, that's not what he wanted. Jim (not his real name) worked out that all he really cared about (his desired primary focus) was making world-class guitars, not all the other things that came with having a guitar-manufacturing business. So he sold the rights to the existing business to a big manufacturer, and went back to living as an artisan, making just a few guitars a year (albeit at many thousands of pounds a pop).

Scaling means a relentless primary focus on maximising market share. Organic growth does not. It's important for you to be fully committed to the eventual destination as you head down what will sometimes be a challenging path to get there.

SUMMARY: CHAPTER 2

- There are two types of growth: *exponential* and *linear*.
- The key difference between the two is their *primary focus*.
- Exponential growth (scaling) is achieved by maximising market share in the shortest achievable time span.
- Linear growth is that which is achieved in any manner other than through a primary focus on maximising market share.
- In addition to the primary focus, to stay alive every organisation must also fulfil a *sustainability parameter*.
- The sustainability parameter for any commercial enterprise is profitability.
- A not-for-profit's sustainability parameter is an excess of revenue over expenditure, often called a *surplus* or positive cash flow.
- Exponential growth can be *planned* or *unplanned*.
- Unplanned exponential growth can destroy an organisation if its leadership is caught unaware.
- It is useful to reaffirm your commitment to scaling in light of the points made above.

Please go to **DoScaleBook.com** to see additional resources associated with this topic.

CHAPTER THREE
SCALING VERSUS FLIPPING

In this chapter, we're going to look briefly at one further distinction. The difference between sustainable exponential growth — 'scaling', which is what we're interested in here — and artificially increasing your market share.

The main reason founders will artificially increase market share is to attract a buyer, triggering what's often called a 'capital event' or a 'liquidity event' — cashing out, in other words.

This is something I call 'flipping' (in contrast to scaling), and the key distinction between the two is that one — scaling — is about achieving sustainable growth over the long term, while flipping is about doing something that is unsustainable over the long term to achieve a short-term goal (cashing out).

The graph overleaf shows how they might look visually:

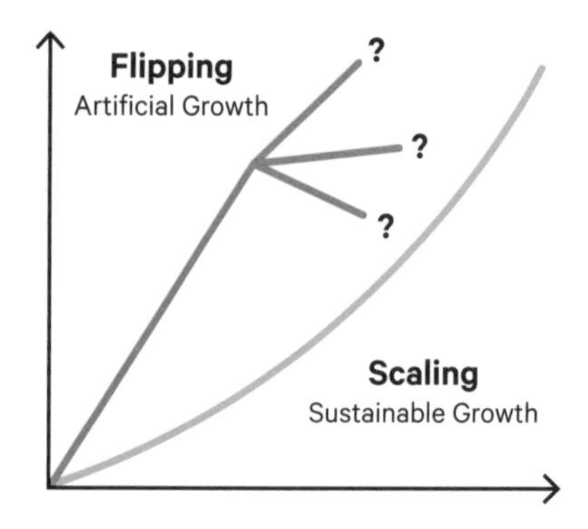

ARTIFICIAL GROWTH ('FLIPPING') DEFINED

You can see from the graphic above that if done 'correctly', i.e. with careful planning and fierce execution, flipping can often outpace even exponential growth. However, as indicated by the three lines with a question mark, the aftermath of artificial growth is much less predictable than that of sustainable exponential growth.

In fact, we can define flipping as follows:

> **Flipping is achieved by maximising market share over the shortest achievable time span without the constraint of medium- or long-term sustainability.**

You can see that the key difference between flipping and scaling is our old friend *sustainability*.

Which posits the question: Why bother? If artificial growth is in itself unsustainable, why do it at all? What possible benefit can be obtained by artificially jacking up market share? To fully answer that question, we must first take a look at how flipping happens — how *does* a leadership team artificially spike market share?

HOW FLIPPING IS ACHIEVED

Flipping is usually achieved by *buying market share*. In a commercial for-profit business this is typically done in one of two ways (sometimes both):

1. By pricing a product or service so far below market value that it attracts droves of customers who can't resist a bargain.
2. By pouring money into acquiring new customers by heavy marketing and advertising, almost always at a net loss (i.e. customer-acquisition costs far exceed any profit on the eventual sale).

The easiest place to see flipping in action is in the tech sector, where literally hundreds of businesses are started every year with the founders very specifically — often overtly — aiming right from day one to be acquired by Google, Amazon, Facebook or some other giant acquirer in the tech market.

Artificially spiking market share for a not-for-profit may seem like a less plausible activity, but it can and does happen — think of mega-churches like Crystal Cathedral that grew at rocket speed during the 70's and 80's in the US (California in particular), largely by demanding next to no core beliefs in their congregation, only to collapse decades later. Or a charity that adds more and more activities to attract greater funding — a factor which (amongst others) has contributed to the collapse of a number of high-profile charities in recent years. Go to *DoScaleBook.com* to see examples of other companies that have engaged in flipping — some successfully, others less so.

Now that we know how flipping is done, let's examine why anyone would engage in it. There are two main reasons.

1. FLIPPING TO ACHIEVE AN ACCELERATED EXIT

The first (and most common) reason to flip a business is pretty straightforward: to make a quick buck (or a quick couple of million bucks) by selling the business on to a deep-pocketed competitor who can turn a profit from the hordes of new customers they acquire.

This is particularly common in the tech field, where a new app, piece of software or computer game can be written, launched and — if you invest heavily enough in marketing — gain a huge following very quickly indeed. The difference in effort required to achieve long-term sustainability by following that instant success with another and another and another hit can be daunting, especially when contrasted with the offer of a huge cheque from a hungry competitor.

A great example is my friend Vijay (not his real name), who emailed me one day to ask if I used a particularly well-known CRM (customer relationship management) application. As it happened, I did, and we started discussing one particular bugbear of using this application — a specific function that it (the CRM app) performed much less well than many of its competitors. It turned out that Vijay was the CEO of a team that had developed an add-on for the application that replaced and greatly improved this particular function — and would I like a free copy? And what's more, would I like ten invites to give to friends and colleagues offering them a heavy discount on the product? I did, of course — and when I asked Vijay why he was being so generous, he was typically blunt: 'I want to get so big so quickly that [company X — the CRM application company] just have to acquire me.' And guess what? He did, and they did.

2. FLIPPING AS A PRECURSOR TO (SUSTAINABLY) SCALING

The second most common reason to artificially boost an organisation's market share is to attract outside investment in order to finance a move to sustainable growth. Think of it as a company 'strutting its stuff' for potential investors, hoping to gain the cash it needs to eventually achieve long-term sustainability.

Of course, the risk involved is that the leadership team is essentially playing chicken with the market: by incurring the heavy losses involved in artificially inflating market share, they are betting that they will attract an investor before their current funding runs out. It's a risky business at best.

One company that did this very successfully is Chicago-based protein-bar manufacturer RXBAR. Here's co-founder Peter Rahal talking about the early days of the business, traipsing around coffee shops and fitness centres in his neighbourhood (my emphasis):

> 'We would ask to speak to the owner and ask if we could put my bars on their shelves. *We gave it away for free.* We didn't care. *We just wanted people to start trying them out.*'

Less than two years later, Kellogg acquired RXBAR for $600m. At the time of writing, Rahal is still the CEO of RXBAR and now, operating with the strength of Kellogg's balance sheet behind him, is head of what has been called 'the fastest-growing brand in the protein-bar category'.

Again, go to *DoScaleBook.com* to see some examples of organisations that have succeeded (and failed) at this.

GROWERS vs SCALERS vs FLIPPERS

Notice that flipping requires a different mindset (and certainly a very different risk profile) than being either a 'Grower' or a 'Scaler'. We'll get much deeper into the mind of 'Scalers' in the second part of this book, but for the moment let's note the following:

1. **Growing** (i.e. building your enterprise for the long term in as organic a way as possible) can be thought of much like someone buying what will become their family home. They're buying for the long term, typically are in no rush to sell, cherish making it into a home instead of just a 'house' — they can often love the building as an integral part of who they (and their wider family) are.
2. **Scaling** brings with it a mindset that is more like that of the developer who acquired the land and built the block of houses — less concerned with the 'homeliness' of the individual houses, and much more concerned with building many of them.
3. **Flipping** involves thinking more like the opportunist who sees a house which can be purchased at a distressed price, tidied up a bit, then sold on as quickly as possible at a profit.

Although these distinctions aren't quite watertight (there are quite a few 'reluctant flippers', for example) they make the point that businesses can grow in different ways for different reasons, most often driven by the fundamental desires and motivations of the founders.

SCALER OR FLIPPER: WHICH DO YOU WANT TO BE?

We've already established that, given that you're reading a book called *Do Scale*, you're likely to be more of a Scaler than a Grower, but it's worth considering this a little deeper. Now that we've seen the distinction between the two, do you really want to be a Scaler, or — at heart — are you a Flipper?

In my experience, the difference between the two essentially boils down to attitude — specifically your attitude as the founder towards detail, complexity and time frame.

If your mindset is like that of a committed property developer — in it for the long term, prepared to do the work involved in scouting for sites, obtaining planning permission, hiring contractors, overseeing the work and selling the final product, then you're likely to be happiest as a Scaler.

If, on the other hand, you have a more short-term, opportunistic approach, and like to get 'in and out' of situations quickly, then it's more likely you'll operate successfully as a Flipper.

Why not take a few minutes now and make a deliberation: at heart, am I a Scaler or a Flipper? And what do I *really* want for my organisation? Either way, you'll find the rest of the information in this book invaluable, but you will, as we shall see, likely use that information in somewhat different ways, depending on your choice.

SUMMARY: CHAPTER 3

— There is a difference between sustainable exponential growth (scaling) and artificially increasing market size (flipping).

— Flipping can be a much faster way to grow a business, but it can be risky, as its aftermath is much less predictable.

— Flipping means maximising market share over the shortest period of time possible without the constraint of medium- or long-term sustainability. Why? Because the aim of the game is to sell the business.

— Flipping is usually achieved by 'buying' customers, either by undercutting competitors and pricing the product or service at a loss, or spending large sums on marketing and advertising, again at a net loss.

— There are two main reasons for flipping: either to sell the artificially-scaled organisation to a competitor, or to attract investment.

— The mindset between Growers, Scalers and Flippers is different.

— It's good to be honest with yourself and know if you're a Scaler or a Flipper, as it will help you best use the information in the rest of this book.

Please go to **DoScaleBook.com** to see additional resources associated with this topic.

MINDSET

The second part of this book deals with one of the most difficult aspects of scaling an organisation: You.

To make the transition from leader of a growing business to leader of a business ready to scale, *you* will need to make some changes.

The Mindset section looks at adjustments needed in the behaviour, attitude and skillset of the founder — and how to go about that.

CHAPTER FOUR

THE MAGICAL STARTUP AND THE MYSTICAL FOUNDER: TWO MYTHS OF SCALABILITY

The world of business perpetuates (indeed, promotes) two myths, both of which are not only unhelpful if you're serious about scaling, but can be considered rather dangerous.

The first is what I like to call the Myth of the Magical Startup. It tries to convince us that (a) there is something uniquely special about being a 'startup', and (b) it's somehow easier to scale a startup than it is to scale an existing organisation.

Brand-new businesses are portrayed as having magical characteristics that will bring great success, if only they could be maintained. In truth, there is only one valid strategy for a startup: *Stop being one.* In this chapter we'll see why this is, and how to make it happen.

The second, the Myth of the Mystical Founder, is somewhat intertwined with the first. This myth attempts to convince us that (a) those who start successful organisations have superpowers far beyond the norm, and (b) in order to scale, you must have one of these superheroes at the helm.

We're all fascinated by 'people myths'. The earliest known writings from the dawn of civilisation are based on them:

The Epic of Gilgamesh; The Iliad; The Odyssey ... All are tales of individuals' derring-do, imbued with one degree or another of near-godlike (sometimes entirely godlike) superpowers. Even today, it seems that every other movie produced is a people myth on a grand scale — from big-budget Marvel franchises to biopics of real people facing incredible odds and, of course, overcoming them.

The business world is no different. We love a business-leader myth as much as any other, and they are promoted just as assiduously. Now, bring to mind your favourite business leader or hero, and I'll bet two things. One, there is a small library's worth of literature devoted to their image and associated legends, and two, they'll likely be a founder.

Founders, like startups, have been given a 'golden halo' in scaling mythology. And in this chapter we'll see why that is, what's wrong with it, and what this means for you if you are, indeed, a founder who wants to scale.

THE MYTH OF THE MAGICAL STARTUP

I'm not sure quite when the business commentariat began imbuing the startup with magical qualities, but certainly by the time of the first 'dotcom bubble' at the turn of the millennium the breathlessness of the prose used to describe these entities had reached epic proportions.

When that particular bubble burst there was a period of some restraint, but this was quickly elbowed aside, fuelled primarily by the re-emergence of, then an explosion in, 'startup incubators' — various physical and online communities dedicated to nurturing and launching startups. Soon the founders — not just of these new factory-line startups but eventually the founders of the incubators themselves — became ubiquitous in business media.

Soon the 'startup mindset' or 'startup culture' — call it what you will — somehow became the gold standard against which every organisation had to measure itself. Books, articles, interviews, podcasts, entire magazine issues began to slaver over the trivial (ping-pong tables and bean bags seemed to feature a lot), the slap-on-the-forehead obvious (it's good for an organisation to stay lean and flexible as it gets bigger) and the mind-bogglingly incomprehensible (failure is really good so we should fail fast, often and with glee).

While there may be a small amount — let's be generous and say perhaps 10 per cent — of the startup hype that is actually useful, most of it isn't just laughable, it's positively dangerous to buy into if you genuinely want to scale your business. Here's why.

THE VAST MAJORITY OF STARTUPS FAIL

Most reporting organisations (like the Inland Revenue in the UK or the IRS in the US) will tell you that the failure rate of new businesses hovers variously around the two-thirds mark — 66 per cent or so.

As a practicing accountant, I learned that many organisations — not just businesses — fold before they even have an opportunity to file their first returns. It's generally believed, and my own experience bears it out, that the actual failure rate of new businesses is closer to 80 per cent. In other words, only one in five startups actually succeed in any meaningful manner.

Now, I don't know about you, but I'm not inclined to view a demographic with an 80 per cent failure rate as a source of role models for business success, nor am I likely to rush to adopt principles and practices that push so many businesses over a cliff in short order.

'But,' you may be saying to yourself, '... all the reportage — all those books, magazine articles and blog posts — don't they tell us what the *successful* startups did, not the failures?'

Nope. Or, to be precise, not those stories that were (or are) written in real time. Here's a fun way to test that hypothesis: Google 'fascinating startups', or 'cool startups' or 'fast-growth startups' — really, any adjective you like — and click on one or two of the articles that come up. The older the better. Recognise any of the names you see? Likely not. Much more likely that they're part of the 80%.

So, in my humble opinion, if you stay long enough as a startup, you will fail too. And we don't want that.

Don't get me wrong. I have nothing against startups. I love them. I lived much of my life among them and have launched more than my fair share. Way more.

Back in the early 90s, I co-founded and ran one of the first ever commercial incubation programmes. It started in the UK and, eventually, versions in multiple locations worldwide were established. The basis for that programme came from my previous background as a serial entrepreneur, having started a number of companies at various times in my career.

I know startups, and the one thing I've learned most painfully about them is that they're a race against time for survival. There's a reason for that massively high mortality rate: most startups simply fail to find their market before the seed money runs out. (The second reason is that they were started by people who didn't have the right skillset, many of whom were lured into entrepreneurship by the very glorification of the startup that we've been discussing.)

Whether it's a bunch of maxed-out credit cards, loans from friends and family, or more sophisticated financing from a venture-capital fund, angel investor or bank, the amount of external financing available to a startup is finite. And if you stay as a startup long enough, i.e. don't 'find and mine' your market, that funding will run out and you will die. Period.

Seriously, the only valid strategy for a startup is to *stop being one*. Many, if not most, startup characteristics are right for that stage in development, but not for scale.

My final plea to anyone serious about scaling their business is this. Don't think there is some 'secret sauce' in how a startup is run that you need to divine in order to scale your business. There isn't. In fact, the truth is quite the opposite.

Sure, there are a few startup characteristics that can help you on your path to scale. Listening to the customer is a good example, as is speed in execution and hiring for performance. But there are many more characteristics that are positively dangerous.

You can't scale and be capricious, for example. While pivoting is an acceptable startup behaviour, it will kill you if you're committed to scaling. Saying yes to everything can be vital in startup mode. But again, keep going with that and it will destroy your ability to scale. Lightning-fast decision-making is possible as a startup because the ecosystem in which you're operating in is (relatively) simple. Decision-making at scale needs to be slower (not slow, just slower) to allow time to gather all the information needed to make a fully considered decision. (Note we're talking here about decision-*making*. As we'll see later, the *execution* of decisions can, and should, still be fast at scale).

THE MYTH OF THE MYSTICAL FOUNDER

Let us now turn to the second of our two scale-derailing myths: the myth of the Mystical Founder.

You know who we're talking about. Steve Jobs (currently a mandatory first on any such list), Howard Schultz, Warren Buffett, Bill Gates, Elon Musk, John D. Rockefeller, Thomas Edison, Ray Kroc, Larry Ellison, Mark Zuckerberg, William Colgate, Jeff Bezos, Henry Ford, Larry Page and Sergey ...

Sorry, I got distracted. It occurred to me that I could just keep going and finish this book with that list alone. We all know the usual suspects. We all have our favourites and those we think are imposters, but with regard to our views on how to lead organisations to scale, we are indelibly shaped by the myths told and propagated about these people.

Here's why that's not just a mistake, it's positively damaging to your ability to scale: For most of us, our perception of anyone who would make it onto a list of Mystical Founders is built on propaganda, not reality.

That may sound like a dramatic statement, but it's nonetheless true. Pick any favourite Mystical Founder and consider the source of your impression of that person, what they do/did as a leader, and the precepts by which they achieved success. What formed your view of them? A biography or two, perhaps an autobiography. Articles on the internet. Podcasts. Newspaper reports. Even films. All of varying veracity and insightfulness, of course, but all of them existing for one purpose: to sell books, online ads or newspapers. And being boring is the one thing guaranteed not to achieve any of these goals.

Profiles of founders must have a compelling narrative arc, or we're going to stop reading. So we end up being fed a diet of sweeping, cinematic greatness and achievement that (perhaps) has a kernel of value hiding somewhere, but which isn't in any way connected to the truth about leading an organisation to scale, which is this:

Scaling is built on the mundane.

The vast majority of the hard work involved in not just growing your business, but achieving that elusive J-curve, is achieved through grinding, blocking and tackling.

Sure, it has occasional big thrills, but mostly it's a daily, hour-by hour slog. It's about putting the right systems and processes in place — and only very rarely about having high-stakes meetings with disgruntled external advisors.

It's about repeating the same boring mantra about consistency and repeatability, and almost never about having a public showdown with your irate co-founder who doesn't share your vision.

It's long hours wading through punch-lists of implementation steps and rarely, if ever, pulling caffeine-fuelled all-nighters at the end of which some inspirational product breakthrough revolutionises your position in the marketplace.

I'm not saying there won't be any drama involved in scaling your business, or that you'll never get to achieve heroic feats. There will, and you will. It's just that neither of them are the foundational building blocks of scalability.

Scaling is built on mastering the mundane, and you need to know that going in.

THE EXTERNAL VERSUS THE INTERNAL FOUNDER

There are two parties involved in perpetuating the myth of the Mystical Founder. First, as we have seen, those journalists who are in need of 'stories with a capital S' to keep us reading, and second, the founder themselves.

Most of the people on our list of successful founders are (or were) well aware of the PR dividend to be reaped by correctly mining the myth of the Mythical Founder, and they did so with great panache. And there is nothing wrong with that at all. 'Rolling out the founder' is a massively important marketing tool. It's used by many companies, not just with the press, but with clients and customers, investors, employees and other stakeholders.

The problem comes when the founder can't distinguish between the marketing tool — acting 'externally' as the founder — and the internal leadership style needed to get their company to scale. Let's look at a few of the key differences:

- An external founder can get to sound and seem all-knowing, with just the right strategy for any and every situation. An internal founder needs to lean on a team of folks who know more than he or she does about their given area of expertise.
- An external founder can seem forever steadfast, rarely showing hesitancy or uncertainty. An internal founder committed to scale faces multiple situations every day in which they won't be sure what the right answer is.
- An external founder can appear all-powerful, with those who report to him or her dutifully in the background, awaiting their leader's voice. An internal founder committed to scale must work collegially and most often co-equally with their top team, rarely pulling 'the founder's card' to overrule others or barrel their opinions through.

FIVE KEY STEPS TO SCALE FOR STARTUP LEADERS AND FOUNDERS

So, what do you do if you are leading a startup, or are a founder (or both) and you truly want to scale? Here are the five key things I teach my clients:

1. Don't believe the startup hype. It's mostly press-generated and is almost entirely antithetical to achieving scale.
2. Instead of revelling in being a startup, find your market as soon as possible and *stop being one.*
3. Be very conscious about which startup traits you choose to keep as you move to scale, and which you need to ditch.
4. Play the external founder as much as it's useful to do so for an interview or investor pitch. Have fun with it, but don't start believing your own PR.
5. Play the 'internal founder card' (using your status to force through your opinion or to overrule others) rarely, and with caution. As we'll see in the next chapter, scaling requires that you move beyond this founder mindset.

SUMMARY: CHAPTER 4

— There are two myths that derail scalability: the myth of the Magical Startup and the myth of the Mystical Founder.

— Startups fail with a very high mortality rate — around 80 per cent. They're not a good source of best practices for growth.

— If your business stays as a startup for too long, it is guaranteed to fail. The only valid strategy for a startup is to stop being one.

— There are a small number of startup characteristics that are good to maintain, such as listening to your customers and speed of execution, but most are antithetical to scaling.

— Most successful founders play an external PR-type role that bears little resemblance to how they lead the business day-to-day.

— Scale-minded founders will rarely play 'the founder card' internally — using their status to force through their opinion or to overrule others.

Please go to **DoScaleBook.com** to see additional resources associated with this topic.

N
E
W
S

CHAPTER FIVE

WHY YOU HAVE TO STOP LISTENING TO YOUR 'GOLDEN GUT', AND HOW TO DO IT

The early stages of your success — the organic growth that is a precursor to scaling — can be, and usually is, achieved by what is sometimes called 'visceral management', otherwise known as trusting your gut instincts.

However, the sheer complexity of a rapidly scaling business will overwhelm even the most seasoned of 'golden guts'. Hang on to visceral management too long, and you risk losing everything you've built.

In this chapter, we'll look at how and why the scale-minded leader needs to learn to trust in *systems and processes*, while not wholly abandoning their experience and judgement. And I'll provide you with five simple steps on how to make this happen.

GUT INSTINCT: THE ENTREPRENEUR'S GREATEST ASSET

There are two inescapable traits of great entrepreneurs.

1. THEY ARE MOSTLY DRIVEN BY A NEED FOR FREEDOM AND AUTONOMY

It's easy to assume that all entrepreneurs are driven by the need for money, fame, or a combination of both. It's also tempting to believe that most entrepreneurs are driven by a burning desire to change the world but, frankly, that's just one more myth that has built up around entrepreneurs over the last couple of decades. Sorry.

While there are certainly some entrepreneurs driven by the need for fame, fortune or making a life-changing impact (and I've been fortunate enough to meet and work with many of them), by far the single biggest driving force in taking the leap of faith to challenge that 80 per cent mortality rate is the founder's deep desire for freedom and autonomy.

Survey after survey proves it, and my own experience affirms that the old adage is right: An entrepreneur is someone who is prepared to stop working 40 hours a week for someone else in order to work 80 hours a week for themselves.

This need to do their own thing, in their own way, at their own convenience and in their own good time (which usually means immediately) is one of the entrepreneur's great assets. It makes them resilient, driven, constantly in motion and fully committed to whatever has their attention in the moment.

On the dark side, this fierce need for independence and control also makes them mercurial, unpredictable, prone to neck-wrenching changes in direction and, at times, volatile.

During the early stages of a company's growth the pluses listed above far outweigh the minuses. The net impact of the visionary leader is more than positive, it is positively vital. Without the entrepreneur's drive, the business will not escape the Darwinian swamp of the startup miasma.

When it comes to *scaling*, however, the entrepreneur's drive for freedom and independence becomes highly problematic. We shall see why later in this chapter, but for now let's look at the second inescapable characteristic of visionary entrepreneurs.

2. THEY GREATLY TRUST THEIR GUT INSTINCTS

Sure, even the most seasoned entrepreneurs can have moments of doubting themselves, even (in extremis) dark nights of the soul, but by and large visionary entrepreneurs trust their own instincts more than anyone.

Those who manage to get their business out of the startup phase, after what were likely many highly existential moments when the whole business could have gone under, emerge with a dependence on their own instincts heavily underlined as a first (and lasting) principle of success. After all, so many people doubted them, so many said they were crazy (likely they said 'brave', but we all know what that means). Others would have flinched, if not curled up into a foetal position, when faced with the same terrifying challenges. And yet, in the end, it was the entrepreneur with the golden gut who was right, not the nay-sayers and doubters.

So now, flushed with self-justification and even greater self-confidence, the entrepreneur leans on their gut instincts ever more, driving the business forward with swiftly-made decisions that are almost always proved right, allowing the business to be both flexible and responsive to customer's needs.

In turn, this flexibility and responsiveness to customers brings success, and so a self-perpetuating loop is formed:

I make decisions based on my own instincts, these decisions are almost always right, and so we grow.

Until, again, the decision is made to scale. At which point, this crucial characteristic — the very 'golden gut' that has seemingly been the entrepreneur's secret sauce — now becomes problematic. To understand why, let's first dissect what exactly we are talking about when we use phrases like 'visceral management', or 'golden gut'.

THE FOUR COMPONENT PARTS OF VISCERAL MANAGEMENT

This 'golden gut' is one of those things that's relatively easy to discuss without being particularly specific about what it is. It's something we've all seen others exercise and the chances are, given you're reading this book, it's a characteristic you possess yourself.

It's unlikely you've thought too hard about what it is you're actually doing when you exercise it. In fact, 'trusting your instincts' is one of the things most entrepreneurs avoid thinking about. It's as if they fear the act of analysis will cause it to weaken, if not disappear entirely.

But to understand how and why dependence on visceral management becomes problematic as we move from organic growth to scaling, it behoves us to break the concept down into four very specific working parts. First, a recipe:

Visceral Management (aka Golden Gut) =
Knowledge + **Experience** + **Insight** + **Execution**

The mix of these four components will vary depending on the decision being made, but for most entrepreneurs there is some of all four in every decision. Let's break them down and see how they work together to formulate visceral decisions that, in the early stages of growth, are almost always correct.

- **Knowledge:** This is the entrepreneur's *information base* — what they actually know about the topic in question. It may be knowledge of a specific skill pertinent to the decision — marketing strategies, say, or how to code; or it may be knowledge about the overall situation — the company itself, or the marketplace, for example.

- **Experience:** Experience is the entrepreneur's *muscle memory*, if you will. It's the degree to which they've 'been there, done that', and have a readily available set of previous interactions to call upon from personal experience.

- **Insight:** Insight is the ability to combine knowledge and experience to generate unique solutions to specific problems. Think of a golfer whose line to the green is blocked by a tree, but who knows from their practice round that if they can land the ball at the top of that small rise to the left, it will roll down to the green *(experience)*, and can tell from their yardage book that they will need a seven iron to execute the shot *(knowledge)*.

- **Execution:** All of the previous three elements mean nothing without the ability to execute. Of a hundred golfers who use their knowledge, experience and insight to work out the correct golf shot to play, perhaps only a handful will actually have the skill to make the shot. The others will envisage it, but fail on execution (I include myself in this category).

Successful growth leaders have all four elements in their toolkit: Knowledge + Experience + Insight + Execution. Now, let's take a look at why this combination — so powerful, even vital, for early organic growth — becomes highly problematic when we decide to scale.

1. THE SEPARATION OF ANECDOTE AND DATA AND THE PROLIFERATION OF INFORMATION

Knowledge, you will recall, is the first element in our recipe for visceral decision-making. And the first way that visceral management starts to turn from a highly positive to a highly destructive characteristic lies in the nature of the information that populates the entrepreneur's knowledge base.

In the early stages of growth, required information is, generally speaking, readily to hand and (relatively) easy to process, facilitating swift decision-making. It's the life-blood of entrepreneurial leadership. During early growth, two specific characteristics of information are particularly noticeable.

1. Anecdote is a close proxy to data

If our sales manager tells us, 'We have a problem with our new product. This week alone, three customers told me they don't like it,' then (at this stage in growth) it's most likely true, and there is indeed a problem with the new product.

As the organisation draws closer to the point of scale and the business becomes more complex, a gap begins to form between anecdote and data. Now, the sales manager's tales of customer feedback may or may not indicate a problem — we cannot know for sure unless we take a more rigorous look at the alleged problem.

Unfortunately, no one ever tells us in advance of this growing separation of anecdote and data, and, having made perfectly good decisions based on anecdote during organic growth, there appears little reason to stop doing so now, until at some point the gap between anecdote and data is so catastrophically wide that almost all of our visceral decisions start to go wrong.

2. The information we need is available in real-time

The second characteristic of decision-making during the startup phase of the business is that, in general, all the information we need (the actual data, beyond anecdote) to make a decision is readily to hand or, if it isn't, we can generally get it with ease by shouting a question across the warehouse floor, say, or texting a colleague who answers within minutes.

As a result, our visceral decision-making can be made swiftly, and in an appropriately informed environment. As I like to say, in early growth a board meeting is a ride up the elevator. You can get in with a colleague, punch the button for the 15th floor, and by the time you step out have decided to open a new office in Chicago.

And again, this is not only right and good in early growth, it's essential. We're trying to achieve launch velocity and there is little time to overthink anything. And it works.

So, guess what? The entrepreneur develops a synaptic behaviour — a heavily grooved, almost knee-jerk response — when a decision needs to be made to make it quickly, believing that all the needed information is 'in the room' and that to delay will be fatal. Which, when the business gets to the point of scaling, becomes highly problematic.

Why? Because in a complex business, all the information is most certainly *not* 'in the room', available at the snap of a finger. It's in databases, buried in emails, and in those lengthy unread reports. And yet ... because old habits worked so well for so long, we keep pulling the trigger on decisions that are increasingly based on less and less of the correct, required information.

2. THE DEMISE OF UNILATERAL DECISION-MAKING

The second fatal blow to visceral decision-making is related to all that has gone before. It's one that fast-charging visionary leaders, driven by that desire for freedom and autonomy, often find very hard to overcome, even when faced with the consequences of not doing so.

Back in the days of early growth, most decisions could be made unilaterally. If the founder decides one bright Monday morning that as well as manufacturing shoes, we're also going to manufacture belts, then manufacture belts we shall! And this doesn't just apply to the leadership and 'big' decisions. Almost everyone in the company can make most of the decisions they need to make in order to get their job done based on the information they have at their disposal.

Typically, in early growth, there are relatively few meetings, and little need for detailed and frequent consultation with others to get things done. Folks are highly empowered and able to 'get on with it'. In fact, they are encouraged to do so. No founder wants to spend their day micro-managing employees.

Yet, as we've already seen, as we move towards scale the business becomes more and more complicated. That complication in turn begins to fray at the edges of each individual's ability to make high-quality decisions entirely on their own. Email exchanges begin. Meetings are convened. Some of those meetings become regular and frequent. More meetings get added. We start to hold kaizen events, install information-management software and find other ways to collaborate. This adds more meetings. We install *project*-management software and try all-staff gatherings to push information around the company. We start a newsletter. And add more meetings.

All of this — all of it — is designed for one specific purpose: to recognize and respond to the decline of *unilateral* decision-making and the need for *multilateral* decision-making.

And in the midst of it all stands our entrepreneurial founder (or leader), continuing to do, guess what? Yep, make unilateral, 'golden gut' based decisions. Decisions that are increasingly dangerous, if not flat-out wrong, because they're being made by *one person* rather than by *the right people*.

Why would an otherwise intelligent, if not brilliant, visionary leader continue to do this even when the evidence overwhelmingly shows that it no longer works? Well, it goes all the way back to what we said right at the start of this chapter: the visionary leader's need for freedom and autonomy. The drive to do things their way, on their terms.

Couple that drive with the fact that they can do it — they're the most senior executive in the company, so who's going to tell them they can't? — and we have a recipe for, if not disaster, certainly immense frustration. With the rest of the organisation working furiously to collaborate, to harmonise, to act cross-functionally, in order to make the best possible decisions, it becomes wearisome in the extreme to watch as, instead, the most senior executive continues to act like a toothless monarch — issuing decrees that have zero hope of real implementation because they're made unilaterally, and take increasingly less account of the realities faced by the business.

In the third part of this book we come to our road map, and we'll look at the *mechanics* of how high-quality decisions should be made in the scalable organisation. But for now, let's continue to focus on the *mindset* required to be a scalable leader.

THE FIVE GOLDEN RULES TO SCALE YOUR GOLDEN GUT

1. Assume that never again will you know everything required in order to make a high-quality decision. Start each non-trivial decision-making process by asking: 'What is it that I don't know about this decision?' A hard question to ask, for sure, but it becomes even harder if you never ask it.
2. Assume that never again will you be the sole person able to unilaterally make a high-quality decision. Start each non-trivial decision-making process by asking: 'Who else needs to be involved in this decision?'
3. Codify, codify, codify. Ruthlessly trap, categorise and store information for easy and rapid retrieval. If it's too hard to get the information you need, you'll go back to making visceral decisions. And chances are they'll be wrong.
4. Decision-making at scale takes more time and is more resource-consuming than during the early growth phase, so decentralise your decision-making by pushing as much of it out and down as you can.
5. Continue to trust your intuition and execution, but only so long as you keep updating your knowledge and experience.

SUMMARY: CHAPTER 5

- Entrepreneurs have two key characteristics: they are driven by the need for freedom and autonomy; and they greatly trust their gut instincts.
- Early on, they make 'visceral decisions' — instinctive decisions based on a combination of knowledge + experience + insight + execution.
- As the business moves to the complexity of scale, both the key characteristics above become problematic.
- This is because of three things: (1) Anecdote ceases to be a proxy for data, (2) the proliferation of data, and (3) the demise of unilateral decision-making.
- To be a scalable leader, apply the Five Golden Rules to rein in your golden gut.

Please go to **DoScaleBook.com** to see additional resources associated with this topic.

MY WAY
HIGHWAY

CHAPTER SIX

WHY YOU NEED TO GET OUT OF YOUR OWN WAY, AND HOW TO DO IT

In the previous chapter we alluded briefly to an important fact about entrepreneurs: survey after survey shows that the number one reason people start new businesses is not the money, but an almost overwhelming desire for freedom and autonomy. This brings with it a dilemma — successfully scaling an organisation requires a degree of ruthless focus, prioritisation and discipline that many would-be scale-minded leaders find constricting and frustrating.

The consequence of this dilemma is, on the one hand, a need for constant variety, the impulse to keep starting new things, a don't-tie-me-down craving for freedom to do whatever comes to mind at any time. And on the other, the need to stay ruthlessly focused on the mechanics of scaling, which are often mundane and unexciting. This leads to a predictable syndrome.

Here, the leader starts the journey to scalability, makes some progress, discovers the need to stay the course on some mundane mechanics (of which more in the next section) and then, in an outburst of pent-up frustration and a need to break outside the box they feel they have penned themselves into, essentially self-harms their own organisation. They tear down or circumvent the very systems and processes they have put in place to build the bridge to scalability.

This whiplash behaviour is not only (clearly) a barrier to achieving scalability; it also, over time, exhausts those working with them. What tends to happen is that the high performers leave to find a more stable environment, in turn making it hard for the organisation to grow in a natural manner, let alone to scale.

In this chapter we'll identify the five most frequent ways in which an otherwise great leader can get in their own way on the road to scalability, and how to avoid letting this happen.

1. AVOIDING CLAUSTROPHOBIA

The core issue for a visionary leader on the path to scalability is to avoid becoming trapped by a sense of claustrophobic constraint.

The feeling of constraint is the visionary leader's kryptonite and will lead to the types of 'self-harm' we referred to in the introduction to this chapter. And the biggest part of the problem is, unless one knows what to look for (and knows to look for it, in the first place) it's hard to detect until the pressure to rebel becomes overwhelming, leading to a volatile explosion, usually overturning a lot of hard-won and much-needed work.

So, what does one look for as a warning that you're on this potentially explosive path? The answer is in the tell-tale 'self-talk' that every visionary leader engages in when they're about to get in their own way, and it usually takes one of three forms:

1. **'OK, this doesn't look very exciting, but I'm a competent adult, I can do it.'**
   Here, the leader identifies something important and unexciting that needs to be done to achieve scalability, which they know won't scratch their visionary itch (overhauling job descriptions, or redesigning the hiring process, say). Knowing that this is needed, even if distasteful, the leader treats the matter much like the need to take an unpleasant-tasting medicine — not nice, but hey, I'm an adult, I can do this. This inner self-negotiation-in-advance is the first sign that you're headed down a path to frustrating and possibly dangerous constraint.

2. **'Jeepers, this is crushing my soul. I don't know how long I can continue with this.'**
   Here the leader is running out of self-motivation to stay the course, and at this point inner resentment caused by the feeling of constraint (at 'having' to do whatever is the important but boring task) is starting to boil.

3. **'This isn't right. We've been successful in the past because I'm a visionary leader and we're not going to succeed as an organisation if I'm forced to be something other than myself.'**
   At this point, the leader is bargaining with him or herself about the now-imminent act of explosive volatility. And note that the inner dialogue is seemingly (though falsely) logical: I'm not being my true self. For this organisation to succeed I must be my true self, and my true self wouldn't do this thing. Ergo, this thing is bad.

Next step: Light the blue touch paper and watch the fireworks.

Which, of course, is problematic, if not fatal, because 'the thing' isn't bad at all. 'The thing' is a mundane but important task needed to achieve scalability, and here we've just taken two or three large steps backwards from that goal, just so the visionary leader can scratch their creative itch.

So what's the answer? How can we break the pattern? Well, the simplest resolution is to avoid feeling that sense of creative constraint in the first place by doing two things:

1. GET SOMEONE ELSE TO DO IT

This could be construed as a head-slapping 'duh' realisation, but is important nonetheless. The moment you hear yourself bargaining in the manner of step 1 above ('OK, this doesn't look very exciting, but I'm a competent adult, I can do it') then recognise that you're probably *not* the right person to do it, and you should find someone else who can.

2. HAVE A SANDBOX ELSEWHERE

Finding other people to do the boring but important things that you can't face isn't always going to be possible, and even if it is, you're still going to have to conduct that orchestra of others. And that can be hard if the piece they're playing isn't a joy to listen to (yes, I've stretched that metaphor but I'm sure you grasp the concept).

When coaching visionary leaders who wish to scale their organisation, one of the first things I encourage them to do is to go and find a visionary sandbox to play in where they can let their creative and disruptive flag fly — without bothering anyone else or, worse, potentially derailing their own business.

And there are plenty of options. You could take an advisory role in another smaller startup, set up and run an event, go on a creative retreat, volunteer on a kids' camp ... do *something*, have something into which you can throw all your creativity and charmingly helpful disruptiveness. It'll keep you sane, and will help minimise those self-harming incidents back in scale-town.

2. DILUTING THE CURSE OF KNOWLEDGE

One of the reasons visionary leaders (or VL) often lock themselves into activities that will inevitably end badly because of the boring-but-important clash is simply because they don't believe anyone else can do whatever 'the thing' is.

'Sure,' thinks the VL, 'rewriting job specifications or redesigning our hiring process may well be something that someone else should do other than me — but who, exactly? No one knows as much about this stuff as I do.'

Well, good point, but, if you'll permit me to ask a question impertinently: 'How's that working for you?'

The logic of 'no one knows this stuff better than me', sometimes referred to as 'the curse of knowledge', is a common barrier to scalability. I'd like to suggest some alternative perspectives, other ways to look at the problem, the next time you find yourself taking on something you know you shouldn't.

Now is precisely the time when someone should start knowing more than you

Maybe you've heard the old saying: If you'd like a beautiful mature tree in your garden, when's the best time to plant it? Answer: Twenty years ago. And when is the second-best time to plant it? Answer: Today.

If no one but you can rewrite your senior leadership job specifications to achieve scalability, then today is the best day to begin rectifying that. Instead of doing it yourself and leaving the tree unplanted, find someone who can become capable of it, and coach them.

Does it matter?

Okay, so you know more about this topic than anyone else, but just how important is that fact?

To give a personal example, when I first began teaching other consultants how to use my Predictable Success methodology with their clients, I thought there were maybe 40 to 50 core principles they absolutely had to know in order to use the model effectively. After teaching the first four coaches and hearing their feedback, I realised there were far fewer core principles than I first imagined. The difference? I discovered that the rest were really just personal preferences.

How many things are you allowing yourself to be burdened by that are really personal preferences, and not core principles?

Hire an external contractor

If all else fails, I'd be amazed if there wasn't someone out there you can hire to do the job for you. And yes, I'm aware that this will have financial implications for the business, but (a) you can't scale on the cheap, and (b) making a financial investment like this is one way of preventing you from blowing up the work after it's done.

3. DECIDING WHO COMES TO WORK: THE VISIONARY OR THE ARSONIST

Visionary leaders have an alter ego, let's call him the Arsonist. We've seen many of these 'dark side' characteristics already. A visionary is creative. The arsonist is destructive. A visionary takes things forward, the arsonist sets things back. People love working with visionaries, they become weary (and wary) of working with arsonists. Here are three tips to ensure you continue to show up as the visionary, not the arsonist.

Have an airlock

Often, external mood-changers are what 'flip' a leader into the arsonist mindset. Maybe you had a row with a friend or family member, or your team got soundly beaten in last night's game, or you couldn't find your lucky socks this morning — whatever the cause, the shift from creative visionary to destructive arsonist is most often driven by *emotional negativity.*

My advice to all the VLs I work with who have started the long and often arduous journey to scale is to build an emotional airlock.

By that I mean a physical trigger — a place, perhaps, like the elevator you ride up in every morning; or a routine, like tuning into your favourite podcast when you get into the car — something that will trigger a reset of your emotional equilibrium.

If you can't fully shake off that sense of negativity, or fearfulness, or annoyance, then at least move into a 'charge neutral' state, where you will consciously avoid acting out of a reaction to whatever is bothering you.

End things slowly

Visionary leaders love to move fast — it's one of the things that gives them an endorphin rush. Discipline yourself to end things slowly. Taking your time over dismantling an initiative or a project or a process will allow you more opportunity to reflect on whether or not it's the visionary acting, or the arsonist.

Think of it like the parental advice you were given about impulse buys. Sleep on it.

Don't make whiplash decisions unilaterally

If you are about to implement a decision that will cause a radical change of direction in your path to scalability, talk to someone. This may sound like a piece of advice out of a 12-step programme (and in a sense it is), but it is both very important when staying on the path to scalability and incredibly difficult for VLs to do. If you're accustomed to following your own instincts, opening up your decisions for others to inspect and critique is hard. But try and do it.

Find yourself one or two trusted peers, and when you feel that sense of claustrophobia leading you to pull the plug on something, give them a call and listen to what they have to say.

4. BEATING THE 7× FACTOR

Any visionary leader worth their salt suffers under one very specific delusion. They think everything happens (or should happen) seven times faster than it actually does.

If a VL says, 'Let's do X, it'll only take us an hour,' you can bet there's a day's worth of work in there (what the VL means, of course, is: 'I'll devote an hour of my time on X before I get bored with it'). If they think something can be done in a day, it takes a week. A week in VL time is about two months in the world everyone else lives in.

This time-warping impatience is, of course, one of the visionary's strengths — they end up inspiring, motivating and cajoling everyone else to achieve what they thought was impossible in the time available. But it's also one of the contributing factors on the path to a volatile act of destruction. Despite the media myths, the fact that visionary leaders are notoriously impatient isn't always a good thing.

Part of the reason is that while it's one thing to put up with (what seems to the VL) the glacial time involved in achieving those things they *want* to spend their time on, it's quite another to watch time being wasted on something they had no interest in in the first place. In other words, anything mundane or boring, aka most of the mechanics of scalability.

So, here's the fix. Continue being righteously unrealistic about the time frames involved in achieving anything creative or visionary (like that new product design, or a new ministry to the homeless in your neighbouring town), but temper your expectations on the boring and mundane (like that new hiring process, or putting in place a customer support offering).

If the thought of something taking seven times longer than you think it should drives you to distraction, then start with a smaller multiple — like twice as long — and build from there.

5. MAKE PROGRESS, DON'T SEEK PERFECTION

Finally, learn to value progress, not perfection. One of the most common causes of volatile explosions by VLs is frustration that what has been built isn't 'gold standard'.

You have a new website ready to go, but it isn't as good as company X's, so you ditch it. The project management and collaboration software that everyone just migrated over to doesn't have the ability to integrate with a particular tool you really like, so you drop it. The beta test of your new service didn't pull the rave reviews you expected, so you move on to something else.

Getting to scalability isn't about achieving perfection. As we shall see in the next section, it's all about making progress over time. And the first step is for you to be mentally and emotionally committed to doing just that: making progress over time, and not starting over every time something is less than perfect.

SUMMARY: CHAPTER 6

- The entrepreneur's need for freedom and autonomy often clashes with the need to be focused and disciplined when scaling a business.
- The need to be focused and disciplined can frequently cause a visionary leader to feel claustrophobic, leading to pent-up frustration, and ultimately a volatile explosion.
- These volatile explosions usually involve the dismantling of potentially valuable and important systems and processes that are needed to scale the organisation.
- A visionary leader can avert such setbacks by, in the first instance, recognising the self-talk that indicates they are on that path.
- It's important to find other people to do 'boring but important' tasks, even if you think you know more about it than anyone else.
- Visionaries have an alter ego, the Arsonist, who is prone to volatile reactions. It's important to ensure it's the visionary showing up, not the arsonist.
- Being realistic about the time frames involved in 'boring but important' tasks is a skill that leaders need to develop on the path to scale.
- Getting to scalability isn't about putting perfect procedures in place, it's about making good progress over time.

Please go to **DoScaleBook.com** to see additional resources associated with this topic.

ROAD MAP

This third and final part of the book lays out the specific road map to scalability for any organisation. We'll discover the 'secret sauce' of scaling, find out why it is so powerful, and how to implement it.

CHAPTER SEVEN
HQTBDM – THE (SLEEP-INDUCING) SECRET TO SCALING

There's a lot about scaling an organisation that's hugely exciting. The sense that you're on a roller coaster, feeling certain you're going to be bounced right out of it, the sensation of your insides lurching as you barrel into another steep banked turn, or the sheer panic when you see what's round the next corner ... Some of us can't get enough of it.

But with all that, the actual hard work of scaling — adding nuts and bolts to strengthen a structure — is most often mind-bogglingly mundane. As we've seen many times, while the media love to present us with exciting stories of steely entrepreneurship, the behind-the-scenes reality is that any organisation that scales successfully does so on the basis of hard-graft, dirty-fingernail, mundane work.

This applies no less to what I have discovered to be the nearest thing to a best-kept secret on the path to scalability. A key skill, without which no organisation can hope to scale and yet, for all its power, is so banal, so hidden in plain sight, that many wanna-scale leaders completely miss it. As a result, they fail in their quest.

To understand this secret of scaling, it's vital to first see clearly what's going on under the hood in the earlier stages of organic growth — not least because, as we'll discover, our 'secret of scaling' is in fact the antithesis of the 'secret of organic growth'.

HOW WE GROW #1: SAY 'YES' TO EVERYTHING

If you look closely at any organisation in the first flush of early-stage growth, one thing will eventually become very clear: everyone in the organisation is making it up as they go along.

Now, although this is a broad characterisation and many organisations become better at planning and exercising control over time, the reality is that most organically growing organisations do so by saying 'Yes' to everything and working out how they'll do it later. In a word, they improvise on the fly.

During this period, there's not a darn thing wrong with this approach. In fact, it's the *only* way for a dynamic new organisation to grow. If you want to gain traction and achieve a viable market share, it's incumbent on you to say yes to everything. Which, of course, means saying yes to things you have no idea how you'll deliver on.

You want 500 cases of my wonderful Elderberry Spring Water? Yes! You want them by next Thursday ...? Um ... Yessss ...! You want them delivered to where? Beijing? Ahhhhhh ... ummmmmm ... yeeeeeess?!?

No matter how ridiculous the request, at this early stage of the business, we say 'yes' to pretty much everything and work it out later.

HOW WE GROW #2: PLAY FLOCKBALL

Okay, now we have a small logistical problem. How *do* we deliver 500 cases of Elderberry Spring Water to Beijing by next Thursday? (Or whatever outrageous thing we've said 'yes' to.)

The answer will be familiar to you if you've ever watched six-year-olds play soccer. You'll have seen how in the early minutes of the game all 22 players (including both goalkeepers) coalesce into a single rolling clump, the ball hidden somewhere beneath their feet, and a dust cloud above them as they roam the pitch with no apparent strategy, going wherever the ball takes them.

And that's how we deliver on our promises in the early stages of growth: we play, what I call, flockball. Essentially, we throw every resource we have at the promise we've made, delivering success by sheer force of will and having all hands on deck.

And there's something thrilling, if draining, in constantly playing flockball. It becomes addictive. No sooner have we somehow accomplished one superhuman feat than we've committed to another seemingly impossible 'Yes', and we're off again.

Not for nothing is this the period of growth when we have beer and pizza busts every Friday night. Why? Well, first of all, because there's no HR Department (yet) to tell us we can't, but mostly because we're reaching the end of every week with a sense of righteous exhaustion. A feeling of 'I can't believe we did that — and I can't believe we get to do it again next week!'

HOW WE GROW #3: BUILD SUPERHEROES

This style of growth — saying yes to everything then doing anything and everything we can to make it happen — inevitably results in developing a culture that commends *heroic leadership*. We don't have time for our people to ask difficult questions or pose a challenge function or even to come looking for answers.

To get that fragrant water to Beijing by Thursday, we need our people to buckle down and just make it happen. Ask forgiveness, not permission; bring solutions, not problems — heck, don't even bring me the solution, just do it, already.

And it works. By constantly saying yes then scrambling to deliver, we develop a Darwinian environment in which there is only room for those who *do things*. There's no room in the fast-growing smaller organisation for hangers-on or non-deliverers. If you're not doing something near-heroic on a regular basis, there's nowhere to hide.

HOW WE GROW #4: TELL STORIES

It's important to see that what is happening during this phase of growth is that we're building the *myths and legends* of the organisation. We're executing tales of derring-do that later will be repeated, magnified and regarded as a Golden Age, when we seemed immortal, unbounded — a time when we could say 'yes' to almost anything — and get it done.

And, in a limited sense, this is true. During this phase of growth we *can* say yes to just about anything and deliver on it. But, as we shall see, there's a specific reason why this is so. And later, when that reason is undercut and our ability to 'say yes and deliver' begins to decline, we'll be left talking about 'back in the day' and wondering, 'What just went wrong?'

HITTING WHITEWATER: EVEN SUPERHEROES CAN'T SCALE

During early growth, the underlying reason why we can succeed in flockballing our way to success is because we are operating in an environment of *relative simplicity.* (I say 'relative', because running any organisation is never simple, but doing so in early growth is much simpler, comparatively speaking, than running a complex scaling organisation.)

Then, at some point in the company's growth — a stage I call *Whitewater* — the truth of this becomes apparent. Eventually, every organisation flockballs its way to a level of success where the detail involved in running things day-to-day becomes overwhelming. We discover that we can no longer come in every day and simply 'make things up'.

We start to make mistakes. We order the wrong raw materials; sign a contract without reading it and lock ourselves into a dumb lease; miss a vital meeting; send a grant proposal to the wrong foundation. The errors, of course, depend on what our organisation actually does, but what's inescapable is that eventually, often over some months, we come to the realisation that this isn't just about a few individuals goofing up, it's become a systemic, enterprise-wide inability to get things done.

To return to our flockball analogy, it's as if every time we look up the ball is elsewhere. Sure, we're running around the field as much as before, but now we're not achieving anything.

To reframe what's happening in a business context, we've reached a vital point in the growth of our organisation, and we need to make a decision. Do we want to rewind to simpler times, go back to being somewhat smaller and return to success by flockballing? (In essence, slow down and return to linear, organic growth.) Or do we want to push through, master this new, more complex terrain, and learn a more robust (and scalable) alternative to flockballing?

HQTBDM – THE LESS EXCITING BUT MORE POWERFUL ALTERNATIVE TO FLOCKBALL

Assuming you opt for the latter and you want to learn to scale, then be prepared to be underwhelmed by the single most important concept you'll need to master. It's such an important concept it has its own unpronounceable acronym: HQTBDM.

HQTBDM stands for High-Quality Team-Based Decision-Making, and you should think of it as the key that unlocks the otherwise impenetrable door standing between mere 'growth' and the ability to scale. To understand its importance, relevance and application, we once again need to look at what has gone before.

DECISION-MAKING DURING EARLY GROWTH

When we're getting a new organisation up and running, decision-making is marked by four key characteristics. Each one breaks down when we grow bigger and become overwhelmed by complexity:

1. **It's mostly unilateral**
During early, natural growth, the vast majority of decisions can (and should) be made by individuals 'on the fly'. A piece of information comes in, the relevant individual considers it, and he or she makes the appropriate decision. Occasionally that individual may consult with one or two others, but rarely do we need to get together in large groups.

2. **Making and executing decisions are seamlessly connected**
During early growth, there's a pretty seamless transition from making a decision to implementing it. Usually the people involved in making the decision are likely in the same room or on the same communication channel as the person who will implement it.

3. **We can make (and execute) decisions fast**
Want to extend our product line to include plastic widgets as well as steel? Make the decision over breakfast, start the process of implementing at lunchtime. Think a second service is needed to cope with congregation overflow? Try it out next Sunday. During early growth, there is little, if any, time between thinking of a thing and doing it — or at least taking the first steps towards doing it.

4. **Anecdote is a good proxy for data**
Finally, as we've already seen in an earlier chapter, during early growth we don't need to go hunting for a bunch of data to support key decisions. A combination of our personal judgement and experience, together with anecdotal 'stories from the field', provide enough information to be able to make implementable decisions.

DECISION-MAKING IN THE FACE OF COMPLEXITY

What happens in Whitewater — the stage when founders and employees become overwhelmed by new levels of demand and complexity — is that all four of these decision-making precepts are tested to the point of failure. Eventually what becomes clear is that, if we want to scale, we need to turn all four precepts on their head. We need to turn all four precepts on their head and unlearn everything we thought we knew about how to make decisions. We need to start doing the precise opposite of what has been so successful until now. Ready? Here's what scalable decision-making looks like.

1. **It's mostly done in teams**
   Unlike in the relative simplicity of early-stage decisions, scalable decision-making almost invariably involves team-based decision-making. Call it a meeting, if you will. The degree to which a decision can successfully be made unilaterally, by an individual (however much of a superhero they may be) massively decreases.

2. ***Implementing* a decision emerges as a process distinct from *making* it**
   In the more complex, scalable environment, the process of decision-making separates out into two parts: making the decision in the first place, then effectively implementing it.

   Often these two steps are taken by different people, and even when they're not, growing complexity means that the ability to move seamlessly from decision-making to implementation begins to deteriorate over time. As a result, we begin to leave a trail of seemingly fine decisions that get *made*, but never get *implemented*

—which, not surprisingly, creates an increasing sense of frustration and impotence in the leadership team.

3. ***Making* decisions becomes slow(er), so that we can return to *implementing* fast**
   As we shall see in the next two chapters, the key to getting back to *implementing* decisions fast is to slow down the process of *making* those decisions.
   Put simply, decisions made unilaterally and in a hurry (i.e. precisely how we made decisions during early organic growth) don't actually work when we try to implement them.

4. **Only data is data**
   One of the key reasons rushed decisions don't work is that we are no longer basing those decisions on valid information. The complexity brought by scaling has severed the connection between anecdote and data and, often for the first time, we need to start gathering and referring to actual, real, relevant data as the basis for making decisions.

Taken together, if we are to scale, this amounts to a revolution in how we address decision-making. It involves building an entirely new skill: High-Quality Team-Based Decision-Making (HQTBDM). The next two chapters will show you precisely how to do just that.

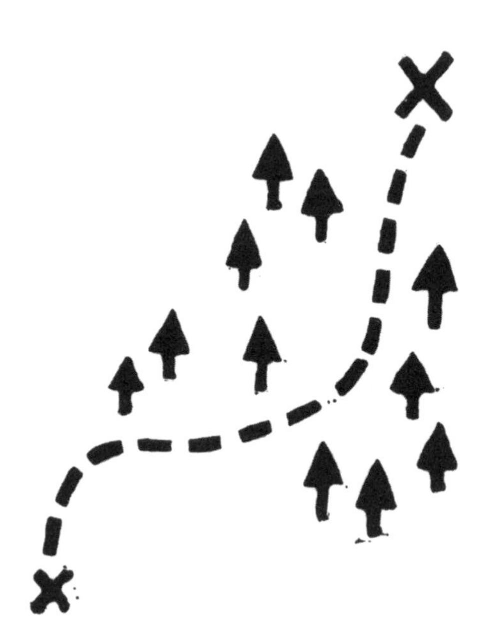

SUMMARY: CHAPTER 7

- During early organic growth we say 'Yes' to everything, then deliver on our promises by 'flockballing' our way to success.
- This in turn develops a culture of celebrating 'heroic leadership' where individuals do outstanding things, often at great speed, to deliver results.
- During this time, we build the myths and legends of the organisation, a seeming golden era when things were fun and we could do no wrong.
- Heroic leadership isn't scalable, and during a stage of growth called Whitewater, the organisation begins to become overwhelmed by complexity, and starts to systemically make mistakes and drop the ball.
- At this point the leaders face the choice of reversing course and scaling back down to a more manageable state, or pushing through to scale by mastering complexity.
- If they choose the latter, they must resist the siren call of the golden era and teach themselves a new way to make decisions.
- That new approach to decision-making is called High-Quality Team-Based Decision-Making (HQTBDM) and involves reversing the thought processes that were so successful during early growth.

Please go to **DoScaleBook.com** to see additional resources associated with this topic.

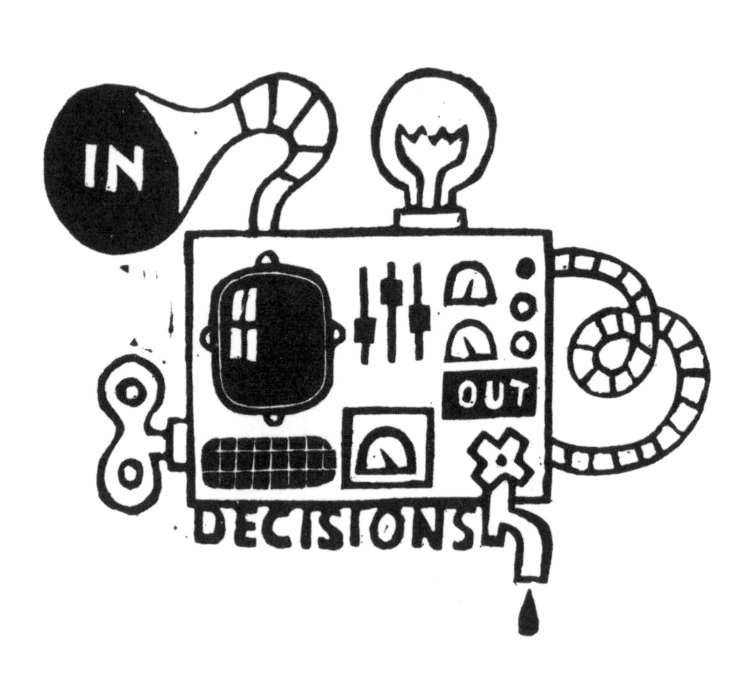
IN
OUT
DECISIONS

CHAPTER EIGHT
BUILDING A MACHINE FOR DECISION-MAKING

As we saw in the last chapter, the single most important skill involved in moving from organic growth to scaling is HQTBDM — High-Quality Team-Based Decision-Making. Within any organisation, developing this skill requires two steps:

1. **Building a machine for decision-making**
2. **Learning how to operate that machine.**

This chapter explains how to do the first, and the next chapter of the book will teach you how to do the second.

WHAT ON EARTH IS A 'MACHINE FOR DECISION-MAKING'?

The underlying concept isn't difficult. If the secret to scalability is the ability to make High-Quality Team-Based Decisions, and if scalability is all about repeatability and, well, scale, then we need a machine that will pump out such decisions minute by minute, hour by hour, day by day, month in, month out, right?

Right. But what on earth does such a machine look like?

Rest assured it's not some soot-charred Heath Robinson (or Rube Goldberg, if you're in the US) monstrosity hiding in the basement. It is, in fact, your org chart.

Feeling underwhelmed? I'm not surprised. The org — or organisational — chart is, after all, one of the least interesting, often least relevant aspects of any organisation's existence.

Patched together over a number of years in some Frankensteinian manner, it usually consists of made-up job titles, ambiguous or non-existent reporting lines, and aspirational job specifications. It is, in a word, dysfunctional.

And that dysfunction, of course, is precisely the problem if the org chart is going to be your 'machine' for decision-making moving forwards. It's the org chart, plus the associated job specifications, reporting lines, information flow and meetings held, that will be your foolproof decision-making machine.

In order to scale, your organisation must be able to:

— **Trap** any non-trivial decision-making need

— **Route** it to the right person, who in turn can ...

— **Access** the appropriate underlying data, and ...

— **Funnel** it to the correct decision-making forum

Your org chart is the machine that makes all that happen. In the next chapter we'll look at what happens *after* that data gets into the right room with the right people. But here are the four areas you need to look at in order to build a robust machine for decision-making.

THE ORG CHART

Pull out your current org chart. Go ahead. I'll wait. I know it'll take a bit of time, it's been a while since you last looked at it, right?

Got it? Okay, now take a long hard look at the diagram in front of you. In your mind, compare it to the everyday reality of what *actually happens* in your organisation. I'm betting there's a wide gap between what's on the screen (or on that piece of paper you printed out) and what actually goes on in your organisation. And all of that guff — the stuff that doesn't match reality — is what's preventing your org chart from operating as a machine for decision-making. And helping this business to scale.

Here are the key areas you need to examine (and probably change) in your org chart if you want to stand any chance of scaling.

THE STUFF THAT'S JUST WRONG

Yep, there's gonna be stuff in there that is just plain wrong.

Maybe you have two Vice Presidents of Sales sitting at the same level on the org chart, one called 'VP Sales East Coast' and the other called 'VP Sales West Coast'. They look co-equal on the org chart but everyone knows that, in reality, the VP West Coast actually reports to the VP East Coast.

Building a machine for decision-making means fixing that. It means having the hard conversation that enables you to restructure the org chart to reflect that the VP East Coast is actually an Executive VP (or, even harder, that the VP West Coast is actually 'just' a sales manager, not a VP at all. (The good news is that the next section will give you a great tool to help you have these hard discussions.)

THE STUFF THAT'S AMBIGUOUS

Perhaps you have a bunch of dotted lines in there — maybe the IT Manager apparently reports to both the VP Admin and the COO (Chief Operating Officer). Not good. And certainly not conducive to turning this into the basis for a decision-making machine. Again, time to pull the cord on ambiguity and sort out reporting lines once and for all.

THE STUFF THAT'S NOT WORKING

You can count yourself very fortunate indeed if, when you look at your org chart, you don't see at least a couple of reporting relationships that seemed a good idea at the time but have turned out to be a bit of a disaster.

Maybe a while back it seemed perfectly logical to combine sales and marketing under a single Chief Revenue Officer, but now you know that structure just doesn't work for your company, or even your industry. Time to make the hard decision and fix it.

THE STUFF THAT'S MISSING IN YOUR CURRENT STATE

This one's easy. What roles are totally missing from your org chart that you know you desperately need? Crying out for a Talent Manager to augment your existing Human Resources role? Now's the time to get it on the org chart.

THE STUFF THAT'S MISSING IF YOU ARE TO SCALE

This last one's a little harder. What roles don't yet exist that you know you will need in order to both scale and then manage that scale when you attain it? Can you easily see the day when you'll need a full-time customer care department? Get it down. Envisage Research & Development becoming a separate activity? Make room for it in the org chart. (**Hint:** Mark 'TBA' appointments such as these by assigning them a different colour.)

JOB SPECIFICATIONS

The second area where your org chart is probably not functioning as a machine for decision-making is in the job specs that underpin the chart itself. Here, one key concept can make all the difference:

Key Concept: Moving from 'Heads' to 'Hats'

In younger, fast-growing organisations, no matter what's written down on paper, a job specification in reality consists of what the current incumbent *actually* does.

Want to know what the job specification is for Tim, the general manager in our fast-growing, five-outlet chain of coffee shops? Walk around with Tim for a day, or a week, and write down what he actually does. That's his job spec, regardless of what any piece of paper might say.

In order to scale, we need to move away from defining job specs in terms of the 'heads' that currently occupy the role, and move instead to job specs defined by the 'hat'. That is to say, what is required of the role to best help the organisation *irrespective of the current incumbent.*

In the case of the chain of coffee shops above, if they are to truly scale, they must redefine the role of the general manager away from 'what Tim does' ('Heads') to what the business requires of a general manager — whether it's Tim or not ('Hats').

Hint: Moving from 'heads' to 'hats' is a powerful scalability step with many additional benefits. For example, it provides a model and the required vocabulary in order to have the difficult conversations needed to implement the org chart changes. It's much easier to have a 'hats' conversation with the VP Sales West Coast about the need to redefine roles than it is to have a 'heads' conversation with Jose (the VP Sales West Coast) about taking away his current title.

INFORMATION FLOW

The third step in building your machine for decision-making is to take a long, hard look at your existing information flow. One of the biggest barriers to scalability is the bottleneck caused by poor information flow.

Here are the key questions to ask:

How is information generated?

It may seem like a silly question to be asking, but if you are going to scale you need to know how you're getting the data that you most need.

Where is your understanding of your market share coming from, for example? Your sales director's gut, or a trusted annual industry report? You need to write down at least the top-ten metrics or information data points you need to scale your organisation and ensure you're receiving trusted, proven data on each (and have each of your key reports do the same).

How is information stored, circulated and used?

A less than insightful question perhaps but the reality is that most wanna-scale organisations trip up precisely because they cannot readily access key data when they need it.

When you're in key decision-making meetings, for example, are people pecking around in their email for that critical report? Or is it stored on a shared drive, in the same folder every month, with a file-naming convention that makes it a snap to find at any time?

Do you have a clear protocol for updating key pieces of information, or are there multiple versions of almost everything on your files? Do executives arrive at meetings with competing versions of the same piece of data? If any or all of these things are happening in your organisation, you simply cannot achieve the decision-making velocity needed to scale.

Hint: The single biggest step you can take in mastering information flow is to get away from email as an information management and distribution tool. It wasn't built for that purpose and it doesn't work at scale. Research and invest in software that is purpose-built to provide information-sharing and collaborative tools.

MEETINGS INVENTORY

Finally, take a look at the inventory of meetings you've built up over the years. Chances are they're a bit of a spaghetti soup, with some being more productive than others.

Essentially, you should be holding two types of regular meetings: *Plan* and *Review*. They do what it says on the tin. Planning meetings are where you discuss what you're going to do. Review meetings are when you look back over what just happened and discuss how it went and any findings. Separating these two is a simple first step you can take in de-fuggifying your meetings inventory, by the way.

Here's a default template showing the ideal cadence for Plan and Review meetings that works for most scalable organisations. List out all the meetings currently held throughout your organisation (always an eye-opening exercise in itself) and identify those meetings that don't 'fit' in this grid. These meetings are candidates for stopping or changing how they're held.

Horizon of focus	Topics covered	Plan	Review
Daily actions	**Operational work** we need to do every day	Daily *'Scrum' meeting*	Weekly
Tactics	**Weekly / monthly projects** we're working on	Weekly	Monthly
Strategies	**Medium-term goals?** *Quarterly to 1- or 2-year*	Monthly	Quarterly
Goals	**1- to 3-year goals** *Usually with an emphasis on financial budgets*	Quarterly	Annual
Company mission, our vision & core values	**The big reason we're doing all this:** Who we want to become and how we're going to achieve this	Annual	5–10 years

SUMMARY: CHAPTER 8

— The first step in developing High-Quality Team-Based Decision-Making is to build a machine for decision-making.

— Begin by understanding that your org chart forms the basis for the machine for decision-making.

— By 'org chart', we mean the org chart itself. The job specifications for key roles; the information that flows between roles, and the meetings in which key decisions are made.

— We need to start by reviewing the actual org chart for anything that is incorrect, ambiguous or not working, and identify any omissions that are needed now or needed for us to achieve scalability

— Next, we need to redefine the job specs and move away from 'heads' (what the employee actually does) to 'hats' (what is required of them for the organisation to move forwards and scale).

— Then we need to review our information flow to ensure (a) we're getting the key information we need from trusted sources, and (b) information is stored and circulated in a way that's easily accessible and conducive to allowing decisions to be made by the relevant people.

— Finally, we need to review our meetings inventory to ensure each one is relevant, efficient and effective.

Please go to **DoScaleBook.com** to see additional resources associated with this topic.

CHAPTER NINE

DEVELOPING SCALABLE PEOPLE

As we journey along this road map, we've seen two things. Firstly, that the key to scalability is developing the skill of High-Quality Team-Based Decision-Making, and secondly that in order to do so we need to build a machine for decision-making. Essentially, a new and improved org chart. Now we want to know how it works: in other words, how it processes information and produces high-quality decisions effectively and efficiently.

Which brings us to the second logical step in our journey towards HQTBDM: learning how to operate the machine we just built.

WHAT NO ONE EVER TELLS YOU ABOUT HOW TO ~~BE A PARENT~~, SORRY, SCALE

Aeons ago, when I first became a father, there wasn't the plethora of advice and information on parenting that there is nowadays. This was way before the internet (it was *even* before mobile phones and recycling). The only source of advice available to new parents was, if you were lucky, a dog-eared copy of about the only book available on the subject written by a certain Dr Spock (not the *Star Trek* Spock — this was a different alien altogether). In short, we had to make it up as we went along, assisted, if we were lucky, by anecdotal advice from well-meaning grandparents. But mostly this was about how much harder it was for them 'back in the day'.

Now, there's a reason I'm telling you this. Even now, learning how to manage a complex, scaling organisation is pretty much just like that. You wake up one morning to find you've got this needy newborn on your hands — and nobody provides you with a manual. It's just assumed that, hey, you're smart and you've gotten this far, you'll work it out!

And so, that's what we do. We work out how to manage a scaling organisation painfully, day-by-day, fighting seemingly unending battles to get it right, skinning our knees and bloodying our knuckles along the way, taking three steps forwards and two backwards until at some point we say, 'Huh, I think I got this.'

Well, guess what? There *is* a manual for managing a scaling organisation. And this final chapter is going to provide you with that manual. You'll be surprised how straightforward it is because it's basically the five golden rules for operating the machine for decision-making that you built in the previous chapter.

Here they are. You're welcome.

KEY CONCEPT: LATERAL MANAGEMENT

Think back, if you can, to the first time you appointed a manager in your organisation. (If you weren't around at the time or haven't reached that point yet, picture the scene. It's not hard to imagine.)

What was the main reason you made that appointment? Essentially, it's a numbers game. At some point a leader looks around and says, 'Hey, all of a sudden I have six sales people. I can't be managing six sales people! I don't have the time for that. I know what I'll do, I'll make one of them manager to the others and she can report to me. Six reporting lines down to one. Boom. Done.'

Think of this — and every subsequent managerial appointment during your organic growth phase — as an example of *vertical management*. These managers are being hired for their ability to manage the people in their team and to take responsibility for what's happening underneath them in the org chart. It conforms to the traditional hierarchical structure of an organisation where those towards the top pass information and tasks down towards the bottom.

When we decide to scale, a new, additional (indeed, over-riding) need emerges: the ability to manage *laterally*.

WHAT IS LATERAL MANAGEMENT?

It's the ability of managers to get in a room (physical or virtual) and make decisions *not* primarily in the best interests of their division, department, project, group or team, but rather in the best interests of the *organisation as a whole.*

This is the single core concept at the centre of scalability leadership: High-Quality Team-Based Decisions are, by definition, those that are best for the organisation as a whole. Not those decisions that favour any one division, department, project, team or individual. Successfully operating our machine for decision-making rests entirely on grasping — and acting on — this concept.

Which, as easy as it sounds, is in fact pretty darn difficult.

Why? Well, think of how the managers in the business have been taught to think up until now. Why were they appointed in the first place? Vertical management — to manage those reporting to them. Until now, how has their performance been assessed? Through assessing their skill at vertical management — their success in managing those who report to them. What have we, as leaders, rewarded and encouraged from our managers? Vertical management — so long as they were effectively managing their direct reports, we were happy.

And now, seemingly out of nowhere, we're asking our managers to learn this entirely new skill of lateral management. And here's the kicker — it's not instead of, but in addition to their existing vertical management skills.

It's no wonder so many management teams stumble when pivoting from organic growth to scaling. Almost always, no one ever tells them this new skill is required, let alone shows them how to do it.

So, for every leader who needs to learn how to manage laterally, here are five key steps that will get you there quickly and with minimum drama.

1. LEARN THE ENTERPRISE COMMITMENT

Here is the mantra of the lateral manager. I call it the Enterprise Commitment:

> **'When working in a team or group environment, I will place the interests of the enterprise ahead of my own.'**

Twenty seemingly simple words. So simple that many leaders will balk at the necessity of having to utter them.

After all, shouldn't every leader think like this? Well, the answer is yes, of course they should, but the vast majority of them do not — and not because they are bad people, simply because they've been admired, praised and rewarded for vertical management for so long.

Write it down. Print it out. Start meetings with it. Learn it, groove it, and eventually, yes, all your managers will think like this and you won't need to discuss it ever again — other than with occasional new hires who come from a different environment and don't yet 'get it'.

2. LEARN WHO YOUR INTERNAL CUSTOMERS ARE, AND HOW TO PLEASE THEM

During organic growth, the customer comes first. And to make it simpler, we clearly know who the customer (or client, or charity recipient — whatever is appropriate for your organisation) is. It's the *external* customer. That person over there who buys your product or service, consumes your offering or otherwise benefits from what you do.

When managing scale, the picture becomes more complex. Stated simply, every growing organisation eventually gets to the point where the *external* customer can only be well served when we get our act together *internally*.

If you're a divisional or functional head, then a key component of lateral management is recognising who your *internal* customers are (spoiler alert: someone you work closely with inside your organisation) — and are pleasing them as well and as consistently as you want to please your external customers.

To give you an example — and this is often one of the first areas in which the concept of the internal customer becomes pressing — a growing organisation's marketing team may need the IT folks to keep the website up and functional in order to do their job of attracting and converting online leads. Simultaneously, the sales team need their reps to be outfitted with working laptops using the latest release of the CRM software. The IT department clearly has (at least) these two *internal* customers who, if the *external* customer is to exist and be served well, must have their needs met.

Do you know who your internal customers are? Do you know what they need from you? Does everyone in your management team know who their internal customers are and what's expected of them? If not, you'll never be able to consistently and effectively operate your machine for decision-making.

3. LEARN HOW TO MAKE DECISIONS

Here's one of those things no one ever puts in that manual to hand to you: How to actually make a decision.

When you get together with your team, do you have a process for the actual act of making a decision? Do you have clear protocols for what information is required, and how that information is put together and circulated? Do you have agreed timings for the discussion aspect? Ground rules for how and when team members can contribute to the discussion? And when you get to the pre-agreed time to actually come to a decision, do you know in advance how it will be done? A show of hands? Majority vote? Unanimity? A 'sense of the room'? The CEO (or whoever) decides?

Remember, when you're scaling, what you have to pump out at a fierce rate of knots are High-Quality Team-Based

Decisions — and if you don't have a specific, agreed process for the actual nitty-gritty act of decision-making, you'll end up going round in circles, endlessly discussing the same agenda items over and over again.

The accompanying website, *DoScaleBook.com*, has a decision-making template that you can adapt and use in your own organisation to bring cohesion, consistency, and speed to your own decision-making process.

4. LEARN DOLLAR-BILL MANAGEMENT

In learning how to make decisions, what happens in the room — virtual or otherwise — is just half of the story. The other half (and equally important) is what happens later once the meeting has concluded.

Time and again I've seen perfectly competent, even excellent teams get together, make a perfectly good team decision, only to have it utterly negated ten minutes after the meeting ended.

How does this happen? In my experience it usually comes down to people. It can be a simple 'blink and you miss it' shrug, a rolling of the eyes, or worse, outright dissent shown by a member of the management team when they return to *their* team and are asked about the decision. At that point, the dissent, however conveyed, effectively renders the decision dead in the water. The chances of it being implemented, let alone fully supported throughout the organisation, have just dropped precipitously.

I teach the principle of 'Dollar-Bill Management'. Once a decision is made, whatever the outcome, whatever any individual team member's opinions or preferences are on the matter — in short, whether you got your way or you didn't — that decision is a *team* decision. It's one that must be upheld afterwards by each and every team member, irrespective of their personal opinion about it.

Once 'outside the room', the entire management team should be so closely aligned on the decisions they have made that no one can get a dollar bill between them.

5. LEARN TO BE RUTHLESSLY CONSTRUCTIVE

This is an important observation of dollar-bill management. At the best of times, it's hard to fully support decisions that didn't go your way. It's even harder if you feel that your opinions weren't heard in the first instance.

That's why alongside dollar-bill management I teach the principle of being ruthlessly constructive inside the meeting space. By that I mean every team member gets to be heard, and they get to express precisely what they think — so long as they are doing so in a constructive manner (non-constructive waffling is not helpful for High-Quality Team-Based Decision-Making).

This principle means that, for those teams that practise it, what normally happens 'in the room' and later 'outside the room' is reversed. And for the better. Instead of the discussion in the room being bland and inconsequential, with the real light and heat reserved for later shows of dissent, instead our successfully scaling teams have fervent, impassioned, few-holds-barred but at all times constructive meetings and quiet, firm support afterwards.

SUMMARY: CHAPTER 9

- In order to practise High-Quality Team-Based Decision-Making, we must learn to effectively operate our 'machine for decision-making'.
- The core concept in doing so is lateral management: the ability of those teams making the decision to do so for the good of the enterprise as a whole.
- Lateral management does not come naturally to most managers, who have learned to excel at the more traditional vertical management.
- The Enterprise Commitment is a mantra that helps managers keep lateral management front of mind: 'When working in a team or group environment, I will place the interests of the enterprise ahead of my own.'
- When managing the complexity of scale, it is important to recognise the concept of the internal customer. Lateral management involves knowing who your internal customers are, and what they expect of you.
- Most teams don't know how to actually make decisions. It's important that you have an agreed process for the actual act of decision-making and that everyone is aware of what it is.
- Once decisions are made, they must be upheld by the entire decision-making team. No one else in the organisation should be able to get a dollar bill between you.
- Decision-making teams must be ruthlessly constructive. This means ensuring everyone is heard, provided they are communicating in a constructive manner.

Please go to **DoScaleBook.com** to see additional resources associated with this topic.

CHAPTER TEN
PUTTING IT ALL TOGETHER

If this were indeed a road map, we'd now be at our 'destination'. I hope that journey wasn't too arduous and you've got some clear signposts about what path to take. So, what have we discovered about scaling?

If I had to summarise a lifetime's experience working with leaders who have successfully scaled their organisations, I would emphasise these key points, all of which we've covered in the book.

- **Know precisely what you mean when you talk about 'scaling'** *(Chapter 1).*
- **Decide early on whether you want to be a 'Grower', a 'Flipper' or a 'Scaler'** *(Chapters 2 and 3).*
- **Don't believe the hype you read about scaling and heroism.** It's mostly about mastering the mundane *(Chapter 4).*
- **Above all, realise that 'what got you here won't get you there'.** The very skills and behaviours that brought you strong early organic growth won't get you to scale. In fact, you'll have to completely rethink many of them *(Chapters 5 and 6).*
- **Build a machine for decision-making, and learn how to operate it** *(Chapters 7, 8 and 9).*

Good luck in your journey to scale. May this book become your dog-eared road map!

ABOUT THE AUTHOR

Les McKeown is the President and CEO of Predictable Success, a leading advisor on leadership and organisational development. He has started over 40 companies in his own right, and was the founding partner of an incubation consulting company that advised on the creation and growth of hundreds more organisations worldwide.

Les advises CEOs and senior leaders of organisations on how to achieve scalable, sustainable growth. His clients range from large family-owned businesses to Fortune 100 companies, and include Harvard University, American Express, T-Mobile (now EE in the UK and Europe), United Technologies, the Pella Corporation and Chevron.

Based in Washington, DC, Les now spends his time consulting, writing, teaching and speaking. Les has appeared on CNN, ABC, the BBC and in *Entrepreneur* magazine, *USA Today* and the *New York Times*. He writes a regular column on leadership and growth for *Inc.* magazine's website.

Les is the author of the *WSJ* and *USA Today* bestseller, *Predictable Success: Getting Your Organisation on the Growth Track — and Keeping It There*, *The Synergist: How to Lead Your Team to Predictable Success* and *Do Lead: Share your vision. Inspire others. Achieve the impossible* (Do Books, 2014).

Les can be contacted at: *lesm@predictablesuccess.com* or via his website: *predictablesuccess.com*

Index

Books in the series

Also available

Available in print and digital formats from bookshops, online retailers or via our website: **thedobook.co**

To hear about events and forthcoming titles, you can find us on social media @dobookco, or subscribe to our newsletter